The Ultimate Party Games Book

THIS IS A CARLTON BOOK

This edition published 1997 for
Parragon Book Service Ltd
Unit 13–17 Avonbridge Trading Estate,
Atlantic Road, Avonmouth
Bristol BS11 9QD

ISBN 0 75252 399 6

Editor Simon Kirrane
Design Pauline Hoyle
Production Alexia Turner

Printed and bound in Great Britain

The Ultimate Party Games Book

Compiled by Geoff Tibballs

Contents

INTRODUCTION

It is one of life's great dilemmas. You've sent out the invitations, spent a day and a half baking enough vol-au-vents to feed the Third World, put all breakable ornaments into the spare room and given the cat tranquillisers. Now only one further matter needs to be addressed before you can be sure that your party will be a roaring success — that is, do you arrange some activity to keep your guests entertained, or simply leave them to their own devices? The latter would be easier, but how do you then prevent your best friend from being cornered by Uncle Sidney and his interminable stories about his career in the tax office or stop nice Mr. Wilkins from the Co-op being eaten alive by man-hungry cousin Wilma? The answer is to involve them in games.

Within these pages you will find over 500 games guaranteed to liven up any party, be it a sedate after-dinner gathering accompanied by chocolate mints or the sort of wild carry-on where car keys end up in a pile in the middle of the lounge. There are thoughtful pencil and paper games; games designed to help all the guests get to know each other; races and romps; word games; saucy games; acting games; and games that are just plain silly. There are games for intellectuals and for those whose only qualification is a certificate for the 50 metres breaststroke; there are games for the energetic and games for those who prefer more peaceful pastimes; there are games for flamboyant extroverts and for shy individuals who habitually spend the entire evening in the kitchen minding the food. Whether you wear a medallion or an anorak, whether your opening line at a party is, 'You've got to be Cindy Crawford's younger and prettier sister' or, 'Did you know this is the driest October for 82 years?', there are plenty of games here to suit your taste.

THE ULTIMATE PARTY GAMES BOOK takes away the pain of planning a party. Some of the games do need a little preparation but the majority require nothing more than a group of willing participants. So that you can choose games which suit the personalities of your guests and their physical and mental state at any stage of the party, a list of helpful symbols accompanies each game. By following these guides, you can avoid creating undue exertion on ageing limbs or causing unnecessary suffering to sensitive souls.

SYMBOLS

A gentle game

Best played after a few drinks

Only to be played when blind drunk

More than one brain cell needed

Intellectually demanding

May upset the neighbours

Guaranteed to upset the neighbours

Danger of structural damage to the home

Physical contact game

Possible grounds for divorce

Liable to cause hideous personal embarrassment

To add a little spice to your party, award prizes and forfeits to the winners and losers of some games. Unless you are striving to impress your guests, the prizes should be cheap, tacky and totally useless — in fact just the sort of thing you find in seaside gift shops. Yet the pleasure at winning a hedgehog pencil sharpener or a set of chocolate false teeth will be immeasurable. Obviously the forfeits need to be tailored to the person having to perform them and to the circumstances of the party. Thus the penalty of walking on hands should only be attempted by the young and healthy and that of streaking across the road and back should be confined to those living in remote country cottages or with at least three members of the local Constabulary on their guest list. More practical forfeits include doing the 'Birdie Song' dance, reciting 'The Boy Stood on the Burning Deck' while drinking a glass of water and spelling Constantinople. The trick here is that the forfeiter spells out C-O-N-S-T-A-N-T-I then everyone shouts 'NO' and so, thinking a mistake has been made, he or she goes back to the beginning. After two or three attempts, the penny should drop that 'NO' is simply a helping hand with the next syllable. Even if it hasn't sunk in, the poor victim has probably suffered enough.

Enjoy the party!

BREAKING THE ICE

Valentines

Players: Any even number

You will need:
Small pieces of card or paper

What better way for your guests to get to know each other than by searching for their spiritual partners? Before the party, the host writes down on pieces of paper or card pairs of famous or infamous lovers corresponding to the number of guests expected. When the guests arrive, they are handed their new identities whereupon Napoleon immediately sets out to find his Josephine while Minnie Mouse hunts down her Mickey. They do this simply by chatting away in character although if a male guest is seen swinging from the light fittings, it is a fair chance that Esmerelda is about to locate her Quasimodo. If there are more women expected than men, this can be balanced out by the inclusion of a Henry VIII or Warren Beatty. Similarly, if there is a surfeit of women, Liz Taylor or Patsy Kensit will prove invaluable. And depending on the nature of your party, you can always use Tony and Simon from *EastEnders*.

Whose Baby?

Players: Any number

You will need:
Guests' baby photos, paper, pencils

Each guest is asked to bring along a photograph of themselves as a baby or youngster. These are then either pinned to a board or laid out on a table with a number above each photo. The players must try to determine which photo is of which guest, writing down the answers on a piece of paper. The winner is the one who comes up with most correct answers. This game is probably best played by a group of people who know each other's names.

Who Am I?

Players: Any number

You will need:
Pieces of paper, safety pins

This popular ice-breaker is a good way of keeping the early arrivals occupied while you're still waiting for late-comers. After writing down the names of famous people on slips of paper, pin one on the back of each player. The players have to find out who they are by questioning each other, but these questions can only be answered by 'yes' or 'no'. Time permitting, the game continues until everyone has solved their personal identity crisis.

Mating Calls

Players: 8-14

You will need:
Blindfolds

Players are divided into pairs, boy and girl. Each couple agrees upon a distinctive ornithological call sign — such as 'Tweet-Tweet', 'Too-Wit-Too-Woo' or 'Squawk-Squawk'. The male partners then leave the room to be blindfolded and, on their return, have to find their mate as quickly as possible. With all the hens chirruping away at the same time, this is easier said than done. To help him, the female is allowed to make her call, but no more than three times. When the pair are finally united, it is the girl's turn to be blindfolded.

Tied in Knots

Players: 10 or more

You will need:
String, scissors

Cut up over 60 pieces of string in different lengths and secrete them about the house. Working in pairs, players hunt out the pieces of string, knotting them together as they go. The winning pair are the ones with the longest continuous length of string within the pre-arranged time limit.

Hidden Agenda

Players: 12 and over

You will need:
Small objects, sticky tape or safety pins, pencils, paper

The host prepares a list of a dozen or so small items — things like a button, a paper clip, an elastic band and a feather. On their arrival, the guests are taken individually into a quiet room where one of the objects is pinned or taped to their body. The best places are visible yet difficult to spot immediately, such as on socks or belts or under collars. The players are then given copies of the list of the items for which they have to search and they then circulate, examining their fellow guests and, upon discovery, writing down the object next to the name of the person on which it was concealed. The winner is the first person to locate every object or, if you prefer a short game, the one with most correct answers in five minutes.

Squeak-Piggy-Squeak

Players: Any number

You will need:
A blindfold, a cushion

One player is blindfolded and given a cushion in the centre of the room while the other guests sit in a circle around the outside. The game begins with the blindfolded player being turned around three times to remove any last hint of co-ordination. He or she must then place the cushion on another player's lap and sit on it. In doing so, the blindfolded player calls out 'squeak-piggy-squeak', in response to which the person who is being sat on squeaks like a pig. If the blindfolded player correctly identifies the owner of the squeak, the two change places. If not, another lap must be found. Once a new person is blindfolded, the players all swap positions. This is an excellent way of getting your guests acquainted and making fools of themselves at the same time.

Blind Man's Stick

Players: Any number

You will need:
A blindfold, a stick or cane

This less embarrassing version of 'Squeak-Piggy-Squeak' involves a blindfolded person trying to identify fellow players from the noises they make. While one player is blindfolded and given a stick, the others move slowly around the room. When the blindfolded person touches someone with the stick, that player is asked to imitate a noise — something like a trumpet, a car engine on a cold morning or a creaky door. The blindfolded player has three guesses at the name of the impersonator. If the guess is correct, the two players change places; if the guess is wrong, the blindfolded player takes up the stick again and searches out someone else.

Cinderella's Slippers

Players: Any number

No sooner do they walk through the front door than guests are asked to remove a shoe. Ladies take off their left shoe; gentlemen their right shoe. When everyone has arrived, the host gathers all of the shoes in the middle of the room and invites the guests to pick up one shoe (obviously not their own) and, in true Cinderella fashion, to find the person whose foot it fits. If there are a lack of women, the sight of the local bank manager trying to fit a size 11 Doc Marten on to the foot of a 16-stone bricklayer can detract from the game's essentially romantic flavour. The winner is the owner of the last shoe to be fitted. The prize is a sip of champagne from the shoe of the victor's choice — but be sure to remove any Odour Eaters first.

Chain Links

Players: Any number

You will need:
Paper, pencils

Prior to the party, write a chain of instructions — one per player. Each instruction has two lines. The first line reads something like 'You are a cream cracker' and the second line may be 'Find a hair dryer'. The next instruction therefore begins 'You are a hair dryer' followed perhaps by 'Find a dog biscuit' and so on until the chain is completed with 'Find yourself a cream cracker'. Each instruction is written on a separate slip of paper and handed to a guest, together with pencil, paper and orders to find the second article on their slip. Players do this by asking each other, 'Are you a dog biscuit?' or whatever the article is they are seeking. If the answer is 'no', the player asks someone else. If the answer is 'yes, I am a dog biscuit,' that person will add, 'Find a toilet brush' or whatever the second article is on their slip. As players find each link in the chain, they write down the name of the object on their paper. The winner is

the first to complete the chain in correct order. The following list may be used for 12 players:

YOU ARE A CREAM CRACKER	FIND A HAIR DRYER
YOU ARE A POTATO PEELER	FIND A DOG BISCUIT
YOU ARE A DOG BISCUIT	FIND AN INFLATABLE DOLL
YOU ARE AN INFLATABLE DOLL	FIND A CORN PLASTER
YOU ARE A CORN PLASTER	FIND A SMELLY SOCK
YOU ARE A SMELLY SOCK	FIND A RUBBER DUCK
YOU ARE A RUBBER DUCK	FIND A CHEESE GRATER
YOU ARE A CHEESE GRATER	FIND A STOMACH PUMP
YOU ARE A STOMACH PUMP	FIND A ROTTEN EGG
YOU ARE A ROTTEN EGG	FIND A TEA BAG
YOU ARE A TEA BAG	FIND A TOILET BRUSH
YOU ARE A TOILET BRUSH	FIND A CREAM CRACKER

Note: If somebody comes up to you and says, 'Find a mouth freshener', it may have nothing to do with this game but more with the fact that you have just eaten garlic.

Chinese Opera

Players: Any number

You will need:
Pieces of paper

On separate slips of paper, write down a line or two from well-known songs. There must be two slips for each song and one slip for each guest. Each person takes a slip and, after reading his or her lyrics, tries to find the other guest with lyrics to the same song.

Pin-up Partners

Players: Any even number

You will need:
A notice board, a sheet of white paper, magazines or newspapers, drawing pins

This adaptation of Pin the Tail on the Donkey is a novel method of pairing off unattached couples for party games. The host cuts out a selection of newspaper and magazine photos of glamorous celebrities (anyone from Pamela Anderson to Lassie) and gives them to guests of the appropriate sex. Each cut-out has a drawing pin through the head and its guest's name on the back. In turn, each guest is blindfolded, swung round three times and aimed at the sheet of paper on the notice board. According to where the cut-outs land, the nearest male and female pin-ups become partners for the following game... and maybe the rest of the evening.

First Impressions

Players: 12 or more

You will need:
Pencils, pieces of card, safety pins or sticky tape

On arrival, guests have a blank card pinned or taped to their back. As they mingle, they write a brief, two or three-word description or first impression of each other on the card. Thus people will be walking around with comments like 'nice eyes' or 'terminal dandruff' pinned to their backs, although it is best not to be too insulting, particularly if you intend staying at the party. After 10 minutes, the host asks the players to read out the card of the person standing next to them.

Soap Stars

Players: 6-12

You will need:
Sticky labels, pencils, paper

Stick a numbered label to each guest and give them the identity of a well-known character from *Coronation Street*, *EastEnders*, *Emmerdale*, *Brookside*, *Neighbours* or *The Archers*. As they circulate, they must talk in character (the host will provide helpful hints if a guest is unsure about the finer points of, say, Percy Sugden) and at the same time try to discover the identities of their fellow players. They can make as many guesses as necessary and when a player admits that, yes, she is Mandy Dingle from Emmerdale, the answer is written down next to that player's number. The winner is the first player to unmask all of the characters. The sound of Mavis Wilton trying to engage Grant Mitchell in intelligent conversation is not to be missed.

Mr. and Mrs.

Players: Any even number

You will need:
Pencil, paper

Based on the long-running TV series, this game can be played by partners who are total strangers as well as by those who have known each other for years. The players are split up into couples and one person from each couple leaves the room. The remaining players are then asked a series of pre-planned questions about their partner, spouse or date and try to answer them in the way they think their partners would reply. These answers are written down. The missing players then return and are asked the same questions. If their answer matches that given by their partner, they score a point. In the next round, the partners' roles are reversed. The winning pair are the first to reach five points. Although seemingly innocuous, this game can turn nasty when couples who have been together for years disagree over fundamentals such as 'who snores the loudest?'

Amnesiacs Anonymous

Players: Any number

You will need:
Paper, pencils

Guests are asked to come to the party with something about them which suggests a lapse of memory — such as odd socks, one earring (for a woman), a watch worn upside down, a shirt buttoned up incorrectly or, for the true exhibitionist, no trousers. As the players mingle, they write down the perceived errors. The winner is the one with most correct answers within a time limit of 10 minutes.

Pairs

Players: Any even number

You will need:
Pieces of paper, safety pins, pencils

This game presents another excellent opportunity for guests to mingle. The host cuts out a series of pieces of paper — the number of slips being equal to the number of guests — and folds each in half. On the inside of each folded piece is then printed a Christian name and an unconnected surname of a famous person — for example Eric (Cantona) and (Benjamin) Disraeli. Each name is then given a number. With 20 players, the Christian names will be numbered from 1 to 20 and the surnames from 21 to 40. One piece of paper is then pinned to the back of each player in such a way that the names are

hidden from view. Armed with pencil and paper, the players proceed to circulate in an attempt to match up the pairs. After asking a fellow guest for permission to raise their flap (who knows what this could lead to later in the evening!) and noting the contents by number, players must lower the flap again in order to prevent others getting a free look. The winner is the first to pair up all the numbers of Christian names and surnames correctly.

Puppet on a String

Players: Any even number

You will need:
Balls of string

Another string game which serves as a good ice-breaker is 'Puppet on a String' although it is not strictly necessary to emulate Sandie Shaw by playing barefoot. The drawback from the host's point of view is that it involves turning parts of the house into a war zone with lengths of impenetrable string wrapped around every conceivable item of furniture. You need one length of string for every two guests. The lengths should then be wound around backs of chairs, table legs and so on to form a vast web leading into an adjoining room. For the particularly adventurous, the second room could even be upstairs. Care must be taken not to create knots, however. The male guests go into the first room and the girls go into the second, everyone taking an end of string. They then set about winding it up until the pair with the same length of string meet somewhere in the middle with a kiss. The beauty of the game is that, if the string has been looped around cleverly, it is not until the last moment that you find out who you are going to kiss. This may or may not be good news.

Name that Ghost

Players: 6-12

You will need:
Sheets, chairs, pencils, paper

All the men leave the room and in their absence the women sit down on numbered chairs and cover themselves completely in sheets. When the men return, they have to identify the various ghosts, jotting down their answers on paper. To help in the identification, the men may ask the ghosts to groan. The ghosts must respond accordingly but must never speak any words. Additionally, the man is permitted to feel each ghost's hair, eyes, nose and ears but, unless it is a particularly friendly party, it is advisable that he restricts his investigation to above the shoulders and keeps his hands outside the sheet. The winner is the man with most correct identifications after five minutes. The roles can then be reversed with the men becoming ghosts.

Match the Proverbs

Players: Any number

You will need:
Pieces of paper or card, a hat or basket

Think up a list of proverbs, one for each guest. The two halves of each proverb are written on separate cards. Thus 'Too many cooks' would be on one card and 'spoil the broth' on another. All of the first halves are mixed into a hat; the second halves are scattered around the house, face down. Players draw their proverb from the hat and then have to hunt out the second part. Only those who are able to produce both cards will be adjudged to have completed the game.

Dingbat

Players: 4-10

You will need:
Pieces of card

A good way of getting people into the swing of things is to play your own version of the popular board game. You need to prepare in the region of 30 cards and illustrate them with picture writing which represents a phrase. For example write a small letter b and a small letter c inside a large letter u. This translates as 'Be seein' you'. Or write the word 'QUICK' immediately above the word 'DRAW' for 'Quick on the draw'. Make sure that you hold each card up high enough so that all of the players can see. When someone shouts out the correct answer, move on to the next card. This can either be played as a competitive game, with a prize going to the player with most answers, or simply as an enjoyable getting-to-know-you exercise.

Matchmaking

Players: Any number

You will need:
Matchsticks or cocktail sticks

Give each guest 10 matchsticks or cocktail sticks. As the players circulate, they take some of their sticks in hand and, with clenched fist outstretched, accost each other with the question, 'Odd or even?' If the second player guesses correctly, he or she receives one stick from the first player. The roles are then reversed with the second player demanding, 'Odd or even?' When that transaction is over, both parties go their separate ways in search of another 'victim'. The winner is the player with most sticks when time is called.

The Missing Guest

Players: 10 or over

You will need:
A blindfold

All of the guests stand in a circle with one chosen person in the middle. That person is given five seconds to memorise who is there before being blindfolded. Everybody else mills around the room except for one guest who sneaks out. The blindfold is removed from the person in the middle who then has a minute to reveal the identity of the missing player. If at this stage of the game, guests are unfamiliar with each other's names, an accurate description will suffice. Should the guess prove correct, it is the missing player's turn to be blindfolded. If not, the guesser has another turn in the middle.

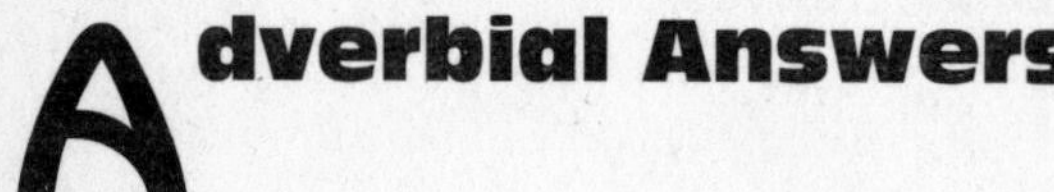

Adverbial Answers

Players: Any number

You will need:
Slips of paper

Before the party, think up a selection of unusual adverbs and write them down on slips of paper, one for each guest. On arrival, the guests are handed their adverb and must spend the rest of the evening talking in that fashion. This game can certainly set the tone for the party as those who have been given 'hideously' or 'aggressively' are likely to have made fewer friends than those with 'delightfully' or 'sexily'. At the end of the evening, by which time 'claustrophobically' has probably gone for a walk and 'murderously' is helping the police with their inquiries, all of the guests try to decipher each other's adverbs.

Find Your Partner

Players: Any number

You will need:
Slips of paper, safety pins

Prepare as many pieces of paper as there are men at the party and write a different male guest's name on each slip. As each girl arrives, pin one of these slips to her back and tell her that she has to quiz the men present to find out whose name she bears. She is only allowed to ask questions which can be answered 'yes' or 'no' and is not permitted to ask obvious questions about clothes, size or appearance, such as 'Am I wearing a balaclava?' or 'Have I got a massive whitehead on my chin?' By the use of subtle interrogation, she will eventually track down her prey. This game is best played with groups of people who know each other reasonably well so that questions can be asked about work, drinking habits, hobbies etc.

Mystery Guest

Players: Any number

You will need:
Pencils, paper

An innocuous game in which players mingle merrily in a bid to find out as much about each other as possible, taking notes as they do so. After 15 minutes, the host reads out a list of facts about one of the gathering who has been chosen as the mystery guest (favourite foods, hobbies, birthday, where he or she went to school, job etc) and the first person to shout out who the mystery guest is wins the game.

Flower Power

Players: Any number

You will need:
Pieces of paper, sticky tape or safety pins, pencils

On separate pieces of paper (one per player) print the names of well-known flowers with eight letters — such as foxglove, snowdrop, bluebell, daffodil, geranium, hyacinth, primrose, lavender, larkspur and marigold. One of these slips is then attached to the back of each player who is told the number of letters in their flower. Their task is to discover the name of the flower on their back by asking fellow players about the letters. Thus a player may inquire of another: 'Do I have a B?' If the answer is yes, that is written down. Even if there are two of the same letter, only one may be revealed at a time and players may not ask the same player two consecutive questions. They must move on to someone else — it is all part of the attempt to boost circulation. Having found all the letters, players sit down and try to solve the anagram, the winner being the first to do so. When playing this game, it is advisable to cover up all mirrors to discourage cheating.

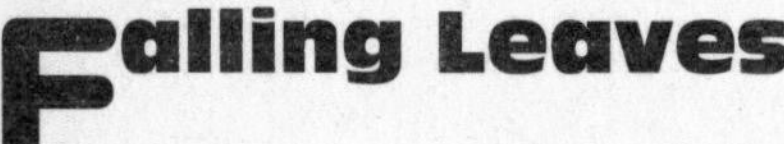

Falling Leaves

Players: Any number

You will need:
A pack of playing cards, two wastepaper bins

The players are divided into two teams each of whom are issued with 13 playing cards of one suit. To make identification easier, it is probably helpful if one team has a black suit, the other a red. The first player of each team stands over their respective bin and holds a card in such a way that its long edge is touching the tip of the player's nose. From that position, they allow the card to fall downwards in the hope that it will land in the bin. After the captains

have dropped their 13 cards, they pick up those cards which have not fallen into the bin and hand them to the next team members. The game continues until one team has safely binned all 13 cards. This is much more difficult than it sounds — unless your name happens to be Pinocchio.

Numerical Order

Players: 10 or over

You will need:
Paper, pencils, sticky tape

Cut up small squares of paper, numbered 1 to 25, and arrange them around the house. They can be secured under an ornament or stuck to a surface, but the whole number must be visible. The players receive answer forms with 25 spaces but each form varies slightly. The first is numbered 1 to 25, the second 2 to 1, the third 3 to 2 and so on to make sure that each player has a different starting point. The object of the exercise is to enter the name of the article to which the number is attached in the appropriate space on the form. The first to complete all 25 is the winner. However the list must be done in precise numerical order. For example if a player finds number 1 and sees number 3, he cannot enter that until he has found number 2, by which time, of course, he may have forgotten where number 3 is. Any player suspected of cheating can be challenged by a fellow competitor and if the challenge is upheld, the culprit loses a mark. If the challenge is rejected, the accuser loses a mark. The challenge rule has the effect of bringing the guests into contact although it may mean that they take an instant dislike to each other rather than strike up a friendship!

Guess the Weight

Players: 5-10

You will need:
A selection of household articles, kitchen scales

Before the party, scour the house for a number of different-sized everyday articles such as a cushion, a pen, a paperweight, a saucepan, a comb and a mixing bowl, and weigh each one. Make a note of the weights and arrange the articles on a table. Then ask the players to write down their estimated weights of the various objects. They are allowed to pick up the articles to assist in their calculations. The player with the closest estimates overall wins the game.

Bags of Fun

Players: Any number

You will need:
Paper bags, pencils, paper

One of the simplest party games, this is nonetheless a hardy perennial. Players are confronted with a series of numbered paper bags and have to do nothing more arduous than guess the contents. This they are allowed to do only by sense of touch. Anyone caught peering inside a bag is liable to be shown the red card and ordered to do the washing up. The answers are written down on a piece of paper and, when the allotted time is up (15 minutes is usually enough), the winner is declared to be the one with the most correct answers. When choosing items, you should avoid anything sharp and concentrate instead on things like a bottle top, a safety pin or nail clippers. Liquids are not advisable either. This game can also be played using a pillowcase instead of paper bags.

Tip the Lemon

Players: Any even number

You will need:
Spoons, lemons

This is an ideal game to play while guests are still arriving. It is a contest between two standing players, both of whom hold a spoon in either hand. The right spoon contains a lemon. The aim is to knock off your opponent's lemon while keeping yours intact. You can have as many rounds as you wish or, for the truly sporting, the whole event can be staged in the form of a knock-out tournament where you will probably lose to the German guest in the semi-final.

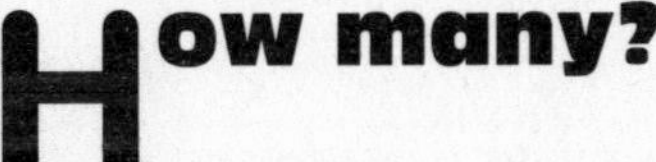

How many?

Players: 5-10

You will need:
Various household objects

In this guessing game, players are confronted with a series of items on a table and have to estimate specific information about each object without touching it or picking it up. This could include:

The number of pages in a closed book
The number of cards in an incomplete pack
The number of matches in a partly-filled box
The number of beans in a jar
The number of paper clips in a half-empty pack
The number of elastic bands in a pile

Naturally enough, the player with the closest guesses is the winner.

Desperately Seeking Susan

Players: 8 or more

You will need:
Pieces of card, pencils

Each female guest writes a brief description of herself and the outfit she is wearing on a blank piece of card. The only name on the card is Susan. The cards are then mixed around in a hat after which each man draws a card and seeks out his 'Susan' from the description. When he finds a likely target, he reads out the words on the card whereupon she will either say 'Yes, I'm that Susan' or 'Sorry, wrong Susan.' The game is over when everyone is paired up correctly. To avoid making the man's task too easy, it is best if the descriptions are fairly vague. 'I'm the one with the purple hair, nose-stud and Mad Dog tattoos' can be a bit of a giveaway — especially at an over-60s party.

Next in Line

Players: Any number

There is no more forceful way for party guests to memorise each other's names than to play 'Next in Line'. The guests are seated in a circle and are asked to call out their Christian names. The host, who is in the middle of the circle, suddenly points at one of the players and demands, 'Who's Next?' If the host points with the right hand, the player must immediately call out the name of the person to their right; if the host points with the left hand, it must be the person to the player's left. The second player repeats the process, pointing to someone else in the circle with either hand. The same rules of right and left apply. And so the game continues at a frantic pace. Any player guilty of going in the wrong direction or forgetting a name is disqualified.

Personal Bingo

Players: 6-12

You will need:
Large pieces of card

Prepare a large bingo card for each player. The cards should each have nine spaces arranged in three rows of three. The players are asked to remove nine small objects from their pocket, wallet or purse and place them on the spaces on the card. Choose a player to start and ask that player to take an article off his or her card, hold it up and call out, for example, 'key-ring'. All players with a key-ring on their card can then remove it. Going round in a clockwise direction, the next person repeats the process and the game continues until someone shouts 'Bingo!' having removed all of their items. If this proves too time-consuming, victory can be bestowed upon the first player to complete a line. To ensure a variety of objects, it is a good idea for the host to ask the guests to bring a selection of small items to the party. It also allows a rare glimpse of daylight for that boiled sweet which has been in your pocket for the past 18 months.

Earth, Water, Air

Players: Any number

This ever-popular game is another good one for getting a party going. All the players sit in a circle except for one person who stands in the centre. That person issues commands by pointing at any of the other players and shouting either 'Earth', 'Air', 'Fire' or 'Water'. If 'Earth' is called, the player must name an animal; if 'Air' is called, it must be a bird; if the shout is 'Water', a fish must be named. All answers must be given by a count of three or the player concerned takes centre stage. If 'Fire' is called, the player pointed at must remain silent. The same animal, fish or bird can not be named twice.

Skeletons in the Cupboard

Players: 10 or more

You will need:
Pieces of card, pencils

On small cards, prepare a series of clues, one relating to each guest. Each clue will offer vague details of a hobby or other highly individual trait of one of the guests. For example it might say, 'Plays in a band'. By talking to the other guests, the players, each of whom is given a card at the outset, attempt to fill in the name of the band and the person concerned. Then they try to find the answers to the remainder of the clues. The winner is the player with most correct answers in the given time.
If there are 10 players, the cards could read:

Plays in a band.
Name of band:
Name of person:

Has a terrible phobia.
Name of phobia:
Name of person:

Is a county sports champion.
Name of sport:
Name of person:

Has been on TV.
Name of programme:
Name of person:

Has a rare collection.
Type of collection:
Name of person:

Owns a sports car.
Make of car:
Name of person:

Has had a book published.
Name of book:
Name of person:

Once spent the night in jail.
Type of offence:
Name of person:

Lives next door to an undertaker.
Name of undertaker:
Name of person:

Left his wife for another woman.
Name of mistress:
Name of person:

At this point it is probably best to end the game.

PENCIL AND PAPER REQUIRED

Wordbuilder

Players: 2 or more

Players are given the same word, preferably something long like 'INTELLIGENT' or 'HYPOTHETICAL', and have 10 minutes in which to write down as many words as they can using the letters of the starter word. Words must be at least four letters long and foreign words, plurals, abbreviations and proper nouns are not allowed. A letter can only be used in a word as many times as it appears in the starter word. The winner is the player with most acceptable words — in case of disputes, it is advisable to keep a dictionary handy.

Telegram

Players: Any number

Each player calls out a random letter of the alphabet until there are a dozen in all. The players then have 15 minutes to compose a telegram, each word beginning with the chosen letters and in that order. So if the letters shouted out were S.S.E.H.I.P.C.E.A.P.A.Z., the telegram could be SEVEN SWEATY ELEPHANTS HAVE INVADED PITCH. CROWD EXTREMELY AGITATED. PLEASE ADVISE. ZEBEDEE. The winner is the player adjudged to have come up with the cleverest offering. An alternative method of play is to select a word from a newspaper or magazine and to build a telegram, each word beginning with the letters of the chosen word and in that order. Thus RESTORED could end up as RANDY EARL STARTS TO OGLE RETIRED ENTOMOLOGIST'S DAUGHTER.

Scribble

Players: Any number

Players are given a sheet of paper and a pencil and instructed to scribble a line of any shape they wish. However the line should not be too long as this can prove restrictive. Having completed the scribble, they pass the paper to the player on their left, at the same time receiving a sheet from the player on their right. When all the papers have been passed, each player draws a picture of which the original scribble must be an integral part. A prize goes to the artist who produces the funniest drawing.

Categories

Players: 2 or more

The players jot down a list of a dozen categories such as Fish, Flower, Fruit, Vegetable, Animal, Bird, Country, Town, River, Boy's Name, Girl's Name and Famous Person. A letter of the alphabet is then chosen at random and the players have five minutes in which to write a word for each category beginning with that letter. For example with a chosen letter of B, the list could be Barbel, Buddleia, Blackberry, Beetroot, Bison, Bittern, Bulgaria, Basingstoke, Bure, Brian, Beth and Beethoven. The players read out their lists in turn. Each word which is not on any other player's list scores a point. The winner is the player with most points. Of course, if you really want to make the game a challenge you could come up with categories such as Characters From Dickens, French Impressionist Artists or British Tennis Champions.

Guggenheim

Players: 2 or more

For those who find 'Categories' too easy, this variation presents a sterner test. A list of categories is chosen and each player writes that list down the left-hand side of their sheet of paper. A keyword of five or more letters is then selected and the letters of that word are spaced out across the top of the paper. Everybody must then write down one word beginning with each letter of the keyword for each category within a time limit of 10 minutes. With a keyword of STRAW, the grid might look like this:

	S	T	R	A	W
Bird	Starling	Tern	Redwing	Auk	Wheatear
Country	Sweden	Turkey	Rumania	Austria	Wales
Flower	Spiraea	Tansy	Ragwort	Anemone	Wallflower
Town	Swansea	Taunton	Rochdale	Auckland	Wrexham
Food	Spinach	Tangerine	Radish	Apple-pie	Waffles
Boy	Sean	Thomas	Roland	Andrew	Winston
Girl	Samantha	Tessa	Rachel	Alison	Winifred
Rock band	Supergrass	Troggs	R.E.M.	Ash	Wurzels

As with 'Categories', players score a point for each word which nobody else has on their list.

Cascade

Players: Any number

Everyone writes down the same word, ideally one of four, five or six letters, at the top of the paper. By changing just one letter at a time, players construct a cascade of words beneath the original word. For example if the first word is 'think', this could be followed by 'thick, trick, trice, price' etc. The same word can not be used more than once. A time limit is set for the game, the winner being the player with most words in the given time.

Transformation

Players: Any number

This game is a variation of 'Cascade' but here the players begin by writing down the same two words, one at the top of the paper and the other at the bottom. Both chosen words must have the same number of letters. The aim is to change the first word into the second word by altering just one letter at a time and each time forming a new word. As a simple example, 'hot' could be changed to 'cab' via 'hob' and 'cob'. The winner is the player who completes the transformation in the fewest number of words.

Players: Any number

This is the ideal game if you are holding a Pythagoras theme party or just want peace and quiet for an hour or two. Each player writes down 13 numbers, from 0 to 9, with no number featuring more than three times, and then passes the list to the player on his or her right. By combining some of the numbers, a new set of numbers is formed, none of which must exceed three digits. Thus if player one chose the numbers 6, 9, 8, 1, 3, 3, 4, 5, 7, 2, 9, 2, 0, player two may elect to re-group them into 79, 6, 8, 133, 4, 5, 7, 2, 20. Taking one starting number (such as 133), player two must use all of the remaining numbers once only and by means of addition, subtraction, multiplication and division, arrive at 666. Multiplication with 0 is not permitted but the use of brackets is. The winner is the first person to complete the equation or alternatively the one who has not lost the will to live by the end of the time limit.

Fire!

Players: 5-10

You will need:
Sticky tape

The object of this game is for players to reveal which six items they would rescue from their home in the event of fire... and why. Before the party the host draws up a list of items, six per player, and writes each item on a separate slip of paper. These slips are then numbered 1 to 6, folded, sealed with sticky tape, to prevent anyone from seeing the contents, and scattered around the house. At the start of the game, each player is given a form headed: 'In the event of fire I would rescue...' Each form is numbered 1 to 6. On the left-hand side is space for the six objects, and on the right-hand side, after the word 'because', is space for the six reasons. Players are then asked to fill in the six reasons... even though at this stage they don't know which items they are referring to. When the forms have been completed, the host shouts 'Fire!' (not too loudly for fear of alarming the neighbours) and each player collects six of the sealed slips, one of each number. Opening the slips, they then match the object named with the corresponding numbered reason for rescuing it. Therefore, object 1 is placed in the space alongside reason 1 and so on. The end results can be quite illuminating. A typical form might read:

In the event of fire I would rescue...

1. The grand piano because I always have it in bed with me at night.
2. My false teeth because they used to belong to my grandmother.
3. My rubber duck because I think it's worth a lot of money.
4. My toupee because it's the best thing I've got for cleaning the windows.
5. A stapler because I've really become attached to it.
6. My pet hamster because I love a tasty snack before bedtime.

Pyromaniacs will probably derive great pleasure from this game.

Word Beginnings

Players: Any number

The host prepares a list of 20 clues, the answers to all of which are words with the same prefix. If the prefix is 'Imp', you could have, 'The Imp that is unlikely' (Improbable) or 'The Imp that you can't get through' (Impenetrable) and so on. Other suitable prefixes are 'Int', 'Dis', 'Pan', 'Sub', 'Mis', 'Pre' and 'Con'. But the word must have a proper prefix. Thus 'Disgrace' is perfectly acceptable but 'Dishwater' is not even though it begins with 'Dis'. The player with most correct answers in a 15-minute time limit is the winner. Access to dictionaries is strictly forbidden.

Name the Noise

Players: Any number

You will need:
Assorted props

The rules of this game are simple — players merely have to try and identify a series of everyday noises. The noises can either be pre-recorded on tape by the well-organised host, or made out of sight (for example behind a chair). The players then write down their answers. The one with the most correct responses wins. Suggestions include pulling a cork from a bottle, rubbing two pieces of sandpaper together and running fingers along a comb. Of course, an adventurous host may opt to pre-record the mating call of the Lesser Amazonian Warbler in the hope of catching everyone out.

The Fame Game

Players: Any even number

You will need:
A bowl

Everybody writes the names of 10 famous people or characters on strips of paper. Fold the strips so that you can't read the names, put them into a bowl and mix them up. The players are then divided into two teams. Alternating between the two groups, each player takes out a strip and describes the famous person without naming them. The other team has to guess the identity. When all the strips have been used they are re-folded and placed back in the bowl. In round two, the same process is repeated but this time players can only use three words to describe the famous person. For the third round, players are only allowed one word of description and in the fourth and final round, the names have to be acted with no speech permitted.

Advertisements

Players: 4-10

You will need:
Magazines

Cut out a series of product advertisements from old magazines and colour supplements and remove all brand names, logos or other means of identification. Numbering each advert, arrange them on a table or board and allow players 10 minutes to write down the names of the various products being advertised. The player with most correct answers wins.

Where on Earth?

Players: Any number

You will need:
An atlas

Using an atlas, trace the outlines of 12 countries on to paper and cut them out. Number each outline and ask the players to write down the names of the respective countries. Depending on the intelligence level of your guests, places like Australia or Wales may be too easy but landlocked countries such as Bulgaria or Switzerland offer a far greater challenge.

What's in a Name?

Players: Any number

This is a soccer quiz in which a list of former English and Scottish League club names is written down. Players have to write what the club is called today. Here are some examples: L & Y Railway FC (Manchester United), Dial Square FC (Arsenal), St. Mary's YMCA (Southampton), St. Jude's Institute (Queens Park Rangers), Thames Ironworks (West Ham United), Pine Villa (Oldham Athletic), Black Arabs (Bristol Rovers), Singers FC (Coventry City), Heaton Norris Rovers (Stockport County), New Brompton (Gillingham), Shaddowgate United (Carlisle United), Brumby Hall (Scunthorpe United), Sunderland and District Teachers AFC (Sunderland), Bainsford Britannia (East Stirlingshire), Excelsior FC (Airdrieonians) and Ferranti Thistle (Meadowbank Thistle).

Stairway

Players: Any number

A letter is chosen at random and the players are given 10 minutes to build a stairway of words, each beginning with that letter. The stairway begins with a two-letter word , then a three-letter word, four-letter word, five-letter word and so on. No plurals are allowed. The winner is the player who comes up with the longest word provided no steps have been skipped en route. For example, if you are unable to think of a 12-letter word your list ends there, even if you can come up with a 13-letter word. A stairway for the letter D might read:

D
DO
DAB
DENT
DANCE
DOLLAR
DOUBLET
DREADFUL
DRAMATIST
DISTRAUGHT
DRAUGHTSMAN
DISCREDITING
DEVELOPMENTAL
DISINCLINATION
DOLICHOCEPHALIC

Nicknames

Players: Any number

Draw up a list of 20 nicknames of famous people and, if possible, photocopy it so that each player has a copy. The players are then given 10 minutes to write down the name of the person next to the appropriate nickname. Why not try some of the following: The Iron Duke (Wellington), Good Queen Bess (Elizabeth I), The Cheeky Chappie (Max Miller), Captain Sensible (Ray Burns), The Rumble of Thunder (Luigi Riva), The Desert Fox (Rommel) or The Italian Stallion (Sylvester Stallone).

Soccer Nicknames

Players: Any number

If your guests are sportingly inclined, get them to pair off two jumbled lists of football club nicknames. Put a list of 15 clubs in the left-hand column and a list of 15 nicknames in the right-hand column. The players have to match the nickname with the club. Try these for size: Darlington (The Quakers), Montrose (The Gable Endies), Rotherham United (The Merry Millers), Millwall (The Lions), West Bromwich Albion (The Baggies), Queen of the South (The Doonhamers), Bury (The Shakers), Bolton Wanderers (The Trotters), Arsenal (The Gunners), Arbroath (The Red Lichties), Exeter City (The Grecians), Southend United (The Shrimpers), Clyde (The Bully Wee), Chesterfield (The Spireites) and Luton Town (The Hatters).

Short Stories

Players: Any number

Players have to write down the longest sentence they can in three minutes using only words of three letters or less. All words must be spelt correctly. It sounds easy but it's not. An even tougher assignment is to compose a sentence solely of three-letter words.

Squares

Players: Any even number

You will need:
Graph paper

This classic pencil and paper game can be adapted into a team contest for a party, particularly when everyone is too tired and emotional to play anything physically and mentally demanding. The game is played on graph paper, and the two teams should have different colour pencils. On their turn, the players simply mark one side of a square. Whoever draws the line which closes a single square wins it and should fill it in with the team colour. That team must then make the next move. The border of the paper is deemed to be one long line. At the end of the game, which can develop into a mean tactical battle, the victorious team is the one which has completed most squares. As a variation from single squares, the game can be played with any shape which is able to be closed with one move.

Squeeze

Players: 2-10

You will need:
Graph paper

Each player takes it in turns to draw a square or rectangle on the graph paper. The shape can be any size, but the borders must not be either those of an existing shape or the edges of the graph paper. Although the rectangles or squares may not share the same border, they are permitted to overlap. The object of the exercise is to squeeze your opponents out of space so that they have no room to draw a new shape. Any player unable to construct a shape is eliminated. When all possibilities — and players — have been exhausted, the last to build a shape successfully is declared the winner.

Connect

Players: 2-10

A series of 36 dots are marked on a piece of plain paper in six rows of six. The object is for each player, on his or her turn, to connect two or more dots with one straight line — either vertically, horizontally or diagonally. The first player begins anywhere on the grid but, thereafter, any line must start from either end of the previous player's line and must not, of course, retrace an existing line. Any player unable to draw another line is out of the game. The winner is the last person who can draw a line.

Consequences

Players: Any number

For this classic game, players are given a long sheet of paper and told to write down certain information. After they have done so, they fold the paper over to hide what they have written and pass the sheet to the player on their right while simultaneously receiving a different folded sheet from the player on their left. Thus players are adding new lines to the story without knowing what has been written previously. There are 13 stages, at the end of which the results are read out... sometimes to the acute embarrassment of those present.

The stages are:

An adjective describing someone's appearance or character
The name of a girl or woman — real or fictitious, dead or alive.
The word 'met' followed by another adjective describing appearance or character.
The name of a man — real or fictitious, dead or alive.
The word 'at' and the place where they met.
The words 'He wore', followed by his mode of attire.
The words 'She wore', followed by hers.
The words 'He said to her' followed by whatever he said.
The words 'She said to him' followed by what she said.
What he did then.
What she did then.
The words 'And the consequence was', followed by whatever the consequence happened to be.
The words 'And the world said', followed by whatever it said.

The end result could be along the lines of:

Varicose-veined
Madonna
met
Glamorous
Jack Duckworth
at
Heckmondwhite's Pickle Factory
He wore a Lycra jump suit

She wore a suit of armour
He said to her, 'Do you think you could handle this?'
She said to him, 'My mother went down on the Titanic'.
Then he did an impression of Tommy Cooper
Then she spontaneously combusted
And the consequence was, they were both picked for the Olympic synchronised swimming team.
And the world said, 'He only wants her for her collection of gerbils.'

Picture Consequences

Players: Teams of four

This is a game for the artistically inclined or those with a colourful imagination. At the top of the paper, the first artist draws the head of a person down to the neck. The paper is then folded back in such a way that only the beginning of the neck is visible to the next team member. The second artist then draws the torso down as far as the navel. The paper is folded once more and handed to the next player, again with only the edges of the previous drawing visible. The third artist draws from the navel to the knees before folding the paper and handing it to the last member of the team who completes the figure by adding on the legs and feet. When the finished drawing is opened out, it may reveal something like a bespectacled granny with a chest like Giant Haystacks, legs like Bugs Bunny and wearing cycling shorts and flippers. A prize should be awarded to the most bizarre creation.

Anagrams

Players: Any number

Choose a category (such as Countries, Singers, Animals, Actors, Statesmen) and make anagrams of 10 words belonging to that category. Photocopy the list and hand one to each player who then has 10 minutes to unscramble as many of the anagrams as possible. Likely anagrams for animals are TAMMEROS, FLAFOUB, ROANKOGA, FEARFIG, PLEATHEN, EGGEDOHH, GREIT, HEPTARN, MALCE and APRODLE which when unscrambled make Marmoset, Buffalo, Kangaroo, Giraffe, Elephant, Hedgehog, Tiger, Panther, Camel and Leopard.

Newspaper Columnist

Players: Any number

You will need:
A newspaper

Each player is given a page from a newspaper and, working from the top of the first column, is asked to find a word beginning with A. That player circles the first word located beginning with A and makes a note of the word on a piece of paper. This process continues down the column right the way through the alphabet except for the letters X and Z. At the end of five minutes' search, the players are given another three minutes to make a reasonably sensible sentence from the words they have found. The words can be used in any order. Any player who did not find all 24 letters has to make do without the missing ones. Players then read out their offerings, the winner being the one who has used up the greatest number of words from their list in a proper sentence.

Dear Daphne

Players: Any number

You will need:
Two hats or bowls

Players are given slips of paper and asked to write out an imaginary question to an agony aunt named Daphne. This could cover anything from fears about your partner's infidelity with the local lollipop lady, to concerns about getting piles. The questions are put into a hat, mixed up and drawn out again. Each player then uses another slip of paper on which to write the agony aunt's advice to the question he or she has drawn. Then the two slips are folded, placed in separate hats — one for the questions and the other for the answers — and thoroughly mixed once more. Finally the players take it in turns to draw a slip from each hat and read out the question and answer. With luck, the advice should be gloriously irrelevant to the problem. Here is an example of the misunderstandings that can arise when two vastly different problems become mixed up.

'Dear Daphne,
I have to make a maiden conference speech next week and am absolutely terrified at the prospect. Can you offer me any advice?'

'Dear Writer,
The first time is always nerve-racking. You may find it best to lie down with the lights off. And don't forget to wear a condom.'

'Dear Daphne
My girlfriend is pressuring me into having sex. I'm still a virgin and am worried whether I will be able to satisfy her. Can you help?'

'Dear Writer,
It is bound to be worrying the first time you perform in front of 300 people, but don't forget John Major used to do it four or five times every day. Take your time, give a slow, purposeful delivery and I'm sure you'll rise to the occasion. And if you're lucky, you'll never have to do it again.'

Battleships

Players: Any even number

The familiar game of battleships can be adapted into a party game between two teams. Large square playing areas are marked out on two sheets of paper, one for each fleet. The squares are divided into 100 smaller squares, 10 across by 10 down. The squares across are labelled A to J and the squares down 1 to 10. Amid enormous secrecy, each team plots the positions of their fleet which consists of a battleship, two cruisers, three destroyers and four submarines. The battleship occupies four squares, the cruisers each occupy three squares, the destroyers each occupy two squares and the submarines occupy one square apiece. The squares forming a ship must be in a continuous straight line — vertically, horizontally or diagonally — and there must be at least one empty square between ships. When both teams have drawn their fleets, battle begins and the players take it in turns to attempt to sink the enemy fleet. Each player fires a shot at the enemy by calling out a square, for example J7. The opposing team examine their chart. If J7 is not occupied by a ship, they call out 'miss' but if it is, they call out 'hit' and say what type of ship has been struck. For future guidance, the attacking team either marks J7 on their chart with a dot (in the case of a miss) or with a letter identifying the type of ship (in the case of a hit). In order to sink a ship, all of the squares which form it must be hit. The game continues with the teams firing alternately until all of the ships in one fleet have been sunk.

Kim's Game

Players: Any number

You will need:
A tray, assorted small objects, a cloth

A favourite game of Baden Powell, founder of the Boy Scouts, 'Kim's Game' is the ultimate memory test and an inspiration for the famous conveyer belt of prizes at the end of *The Generation Game*. Place in the region of 20 different small objects on a tray (things like a clothes peg, an elastic band, a corkscrew and a pair of scissors) and cover the tray with a cloth. Then gather the players around the tray and remove the cloth for 30 seconds. After replacing the cloth, ask the players to write down as many objects as they can remember in five minutes. Players score a point for every item they remember but lose a point if they name an object which was not on the tray. The player with most points is declared the victor.

The Trick Tray

Players: Any number

You will need:
A tray, assorted small objects, a cloth

This is an even more cunning variation of 'Kim's Game'. The host's assistant (it could be one of his children or a neighbour) removes the cloth to enable the players to examine the tray of objects for 30 seconds. But the catch comes just as the assistant leaves the room with the tray. The players are told that, instead of writing down a list of the items on the tray, they have to try to remember as many things as they can about the assistant — such as clothing, hair colour and jewellery etc.

Prefixes

Players: Any number

This alternative to 'Word Beginnings' does not involve clues but instead requires players to name as many words as they can with a given prefix in 20 minutes.

What's Missing?

Players; Any number

You will need:
A tray, assorted small objects, a cloth

In this variation of 'Kim's Game', the players gather round to study the 20 or so items on the tray for a period of 30 seconds. The cloth is then replaced and the host surreptitiously removes one article. The cloth is then removed again and the players have to write down which item has vanished. The routine is repeated over 10 rounds with one object being removed each time. After each round, the articles should be moved around a little to stop the players becoming too familiar with their whereabouts. Also a devious host may opt to remove the same item for two successive rounds. At the end of the 10 rounds, the player with most right answers is the winner.

Political Correctness

Players: Any number

In the age of political correctness comes the eternal quest for yet more convoluted phrases to replace seemingly innocuous everyday words. Now that 'short' is 'vertically challenged' and 'poor' is 'economically disadvantaged', it can be fun trying to think up ridiculous PC alternatives for other adjectives. So see who can write down the best translation for the following: bow-legged, stupid, ignorant, jug-eared, repulsive, lazy, pig-headed, two-faced, homicidal, drunk, randy and foul-mouthed. If all of these apply to one of your guests, assure him or her that your choice of words was purely coincidental.

Three-Word Verses

Players: Any number

You will need:
A hat or a bowl

Each player writes three words on separate pieces of paper. These are then folded and put into a hat or a bowl. The slips are shuffled and each player draws out three. The aim is to compose a four-line rhyme incorporating all three words in any order. Obviously this is not too demanding if the words are something like 'pretty', 'girl' and 'blue', but it is quite a different matter with 'dodecahedron', 'liquescent' and 'prestidigitator'.

Animal Answers

Players: Any number

Think of a dozen words containing the name of an animal (*Ant*arctic, *Fox*glove, *Lion*ise, *Stag*nation, Lic*hen* etc) and write down a definition for each one. Give a copy of the list of definitions to each player and allow them 10 minutes to fill in the animals concerned.

Hidden Quadrupeds

Players: Any number

Another game where the names of animals are hidden, but this time in sentences. Try your guests with the following and see whether they can spot all the animals in two minutes.

In America the most popular sport is baseball.
The forecast says it will be a very hot day.
The defendant insisted there was nothing to add.
When the sergeant arrives, the private jumps to attention.
We heard the band in good form.
In the bathroom there is soap and a towel.
Which are the principal ports of Belgium?
A voice called out, 'Do get a move on!'
To span the river, the locals built a fine bridge.
If the robber is caught there will be a reward.

Answers: 1. Cat 2. Beaver 3. Toad 4. Stoat 5. Dingo 6. Panda 7. Hare 8. Dog 9. Panther 10. Bear

The game can also be played with other subjects such as birds, flowers, towns and trees.

Drawing in the Dark

Players: 2-6

You will need:
Blindfolds

Players are blindfolded and asked to draw a picture of their house, adding on such accessories as a car, a few flowers and trees, clouds in the sky and perhaps even a passing postman and dog. When the drawings are finished, the blindfolds are removed and the fascinating results examined.

Name the Tune

Players: Any number

You will need:
A tape recorder

Before the party, compile a tape featuring a few bars of a dozen songs, following on quickly one after another. Give each player pencil and paper and switch on the tape. Ask them to write down as many titles as they can recognise, the winner being the one with most correct answers. Unless your party is composed of record producers and rock stars, it is only fair to make most of the tracks fairly distinctive although it is always tempting to slip in a Moira Anderson album track to sort out the men from the boys.

Pick a Letter

Players: Any number

Select a letter and get the players to go through the alphabet writing down pairs of connected words, the second word of which must always begin with the chosen letter. Thus if the letter is S, the list could be:

Able Seaman
Brain Surgeon
Calcium Sulphate
Dover Sole
Extra Sensory
Film Star
Gordon Sumner (aka Sting)
Hazy Sunshine
Ink Spots
Jay Silverheels (who played Tonto in *The Lone Ranger*)
King Solomon
Leather Shoes
Milk Shake
Night Shirt
Open Sesame
Prime Suspect
Quiz Show
Rail Strike
Smoked Salmon
Tom Sawyer
Urine Sample
Virtual Standstill
Word Search
Xmas Spread
Yard Stick
Zebra Stripes

At the end of the 10-minute time limit, players read out their lists and delete any answers that have already been given. The player with the greatest number of original pairings is declared the winner.

Lovely Words

Players: Any number

Players are given five minutes to write down as many English language words as possible which contain the word 'love' ('clover, glove, plover, lovely, slovenly, beloved, lovelorn' etc). When the lists are read, each player checks their answers for duplicates. A player with a word not on anyone else's list scores a point, the winner being the one with most points.

Singing Charades

Players: Any even number up to 12

'Singing Charades' requires players to guess song titles depicted in drawings. Guests are divided into two teams of five or six each and one person from each team goes forward to receive the title of a song from the host. Those two players then go back to their respective teams and draw a picture which suggests the title. No words can be spoken or written by the artist. The first team to guess the right answer and sing the song (not in its entirety) wins. The game continues until every player has had a turn at being the artist. The following titles can make for an interesting — if lengthy — encounter:
'The Lunatics Have Taken Over the Asylum'
'Calling Occupants of Interplanetary Craft'
'Does Your Chewing Gum Lose Its Flavour (on the Bedpost Overnight)?'
'Gilly Gilly Ossenfeffer Katzenellen Bogen By The Sea'
'I Saw Mommy Kissing Santa Claus'
'My Boomerang Won't Come Back'
'Subterranean Homesick Blues'
'Wombling Merry Christmas'
'Boom Bang-a-Bang'

Sales Promotion

Players: 5-10

Here is a game for would-be advertising copywriters, the sort of people who lie awake at night trying to think up a catchy slogan for corn plasters. Players are asked to fill in a form promoting the virtues of a new product... without actually knowing what the product is. Beforehand, the host draws up the form with spaces for the brand name of the article, what it is made of, when and how to use it, its promotional slogan and the name of a celebrity who swears by it. A copy of the form is handed to each player who uses his or her imagination to come up with some suitable answers — the more bizarre the better. When all of the forms are completed, players are given a card bearing the name of the product which they are supposed to be promoting. This name is added to their form in the space for Article. Then each player reads out their finished form. A typical example might be:

Brand name: Whizzo

Article: Nostril-hair removal cream

Made of: Sun-ripe tomatoes, mangos and pineapple

When to use: Only during a full moon

How to use: Dip the affected area in concentrated sulphuric acid

Slogan: You'll feel twice the man with Whizzo

Celebrity who uses it: Attila the Hun

Other articles which may prove useful for this game include: Drain-clearing rods, toupee, thermometer, pneumatic drill, soldering iron, dental floss, circular saw, carving knife and a pair of Y-fronts.

Crosswords

Players: 5 or more

Crossword buffs will enjoy this opportunity to create their own puzzle even though the finished product may not be quite as complex as the one they are used to doing on the 8.22 to Waterloo. Before the game starts, each player has to draw a grid of squares — the same number across as down — on a sheet of paper. The size of the grid depends upon the number of players. For five players, seven squares across and seven down is ideal, but with more participants a bigger grid is necessary. Each player in turn then calls out any letter of his or her choice whereupon the other players must enter that letter somewhere in their own grids. Once that letter has been entered, it cannot be moved. The object of the game is to form words either across or down, the game finishing when all of the squares have been filled. One point is scored for each letter in an acceptable word — abbreviations, proper nouns, one-letter words and foreign words do not count. A letter may not be shared by two or more words in the same line or column. For example, if a player's line reads RAMPSTO, the maximum number of points he or she can score for that line is five for RAMPS. There are no extra points for RAM, AMP or AMPS. If a player has a word which fills an entire row or column, he or she receives a bonus point. The player with the highest total score is the winner. For example:

R	O	U	N	D	L	Y	8
A	N	K	L	E	F	X	5
N	E	B	O	A	K	T	6
C	W	L	Z	D	M	H	0
H	A	L	F	I	N	D	6
B	I	T	G	P	S	O	5
L	T	O	N	G	U	E	6
5	7	2	0	4	0	3	3

Total: 57

The Lyric Game

Players: Any even number

Before the party, go through your collection of CDs and old vinyl and write down two lines of lyrics from a dozen different songs. It is best to stick to songs which have actually been hits and to bear in mind the age range of your guests. There is little point in including Blur or Oasis tracks at an OAPs gathering while conversely the classic Major Lance lyrics 'Um um um um um um' from 1964 will be wasted at a party where the oldest guest is 25. Players are divided into two teams and the first team to guess the name of the tune from which the lyrics are taken and the artist who recorded it scores two points. If a team only gets half the answer right, they score one point. Be prepared for a great deal of argument and shouts of, 'That was never from "Agadoo"!'

Four-Letter Words

Players: 5-10

This game involves players trying to work out a rival's chosen keyword by a process of elimination. Each player chooses a four-letter word and writes it down without letting any of the other competitors see it (this is to prevent players illegally changing their word mid-way through the game). Going in a clockwise direction, players take it in turns to try to discover the chosen word of the player on their left by coming up with a succession of guess words. If player one has selected MASH as his or her keyword and player two volunteers CALF as his or guess word, player one must respond with how many letters in the guess word correspond to those of the keyword. In this instance, the only letter featured in both words is an 'A' so the reply would be one letter. Whilst player two is trying to ascertain player one's keyword, player three is attempting to discover player two's and so on. If a player has chosen a keyword with a double or treble letter (such as TWIT or EPEE), his or her reply to the guess word must reveal how many letters have been scored out of the four, including duplicates. So with a keyword of EPEE and a guess word of HATE, the answer would be three letters as there are three Es in the keyword. The trick is to find out whether the 'three' refers to three different letters, two the same or three the same. Thus testing for duplicates is all important. Artful players often prefer to choose anagrams as their keywords. With MASH, player two might have discovered all of the letters, but he or she still has to get them in the right order. For the keyword could also be SHAM. The extra go needed to solve that problem could allow another player to win.

Scaffold

Players: Any number

Each player is given the same three letters of the alphabet picked at random from a newspaper and has 10 minutes in which to think of as many words as possible featuring those three letters in the order given. Players score a point for each word but no plurals are allowed. For example, if the letters selected are P,R and S, among the eligible words are: Purse, Pursue, Praise, Perish, Parish, Persecute, Prose, Appraise, Sparse, Parsnip, Parsimony, Persist, Press, Suppress, Surprise, Precious, Pernicious, Reprise, Person, Personally, Personification, Persuasion, Persevere, Parsonage, Parsley, Prosaic, Process and Priest. For those seeking a tougher challenge, try playing the game with four selected letters, such as M, N, T, Y which could yield Minty, Monetary, Monthly, Elementary, Amnesty, Mandatory, Misanthropy etc.

Hollywood Trailers

Players: 5-10

You will need:
A hat or a bowl

The American movie industry is not in the habit of underselling anything — they would make a screen version of the Vauxhall Nova car manual sound like the greatest story ever told if they thought it would make a buck or two! So here is a chance for each of your guests to don the mantle of a Hollywood trailer writer by composing short, snappy, sensational pieces to promote a new film adaptation of a classic book. Prepare a selection of titles, each on a separate slip of paper, and mix them up in a hat or bowl. Ask each player to draw a slip and give them five minutes to write their pieces. The most ingenious trailer wins a prize. Here are a few books which have inexplicably escaped the clutches of Hollywood to date, but which might be ripe for the big screen:

The Concise Oxford Dictionary
Knitting for Beginners
The South Lincolnshire Telephone Directory
Modern Sewage Methods
101 Things to do with Raffia
The Goldfish — a History

Terminations

Players: Any number

The host draws up a list of 20 words ending in the word 'nation' and supplies clues for each word. Each player is given a copy of the list and has to fill in the answers in 10 minutes, the one with most correct replies being the winner. Examples include:

The nation of light (illumination)
The nation of political murder (assassination)
The nation of clove-scented flowers (carnation)
The nation of explosion (detonation)
The nation of riddance (elimination)
The nation of journey's end (destination)

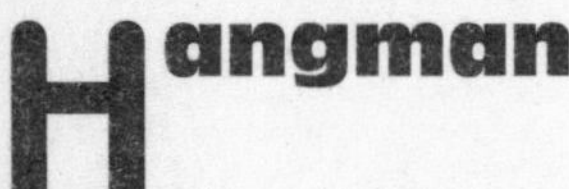

Hangman

Players: Any even number

Habitually played at school during boring maths lessons while the teacher's back is turned, 'Hangman' makes a good team party game. The aim is simple — to try and guess the other team's word in fewer than 11 attempts. The first team think of a word and write down a series of dashes, one for each letter. The second team then starts guessing the letters in the word, calling out one at a time. If the letter occurs in the word, it is written above the appropriate dash. If the same letter appears more than once in the word, every occurrence must be noted. Thus if you call out an E and the word is ESSENTIAL, two Es will be put in the correct spaces. If the second team's letter does not occur in the word, the first team draw part of the Hangman picture, depicting a hapless individual on the scaffold. There are 11 sections in all — base, upright, crosspiece, support, rope, head, body, left arm, right arm, left leg and right leg — and they must be drawn in that order. Should the first team complete the picture before the word is guessed, they win the game. To avoid repetition, all incorrect letter guesses are recorded beneath the dashes. It is worth remembering that shorter words like ORYX, ZEBU or LYNX are more likely to result in the successful hanging of your opponent.

Cities

Players: Any number

Prepare a list of clues for 20 words ending with the word 'city' and ask the players to fill in the answers within a 10-minute time limit. Listed below are a few suggestions:

The city of bizarre behaviour (eccentricity)
The city of speed (velocity)
The city of wisdom (sagacity)
The city of deception (duplicity)
The city of currents (electricity)
The city of numbers (multiplicity)

Combinations

Players: Any number

If you feel your party is degenerating towards tabloid sleaze, here is a game guaranteed to raise the tone. Strictly for spelling experts, it requires players to find words containing various combinations of letters. First draw up a list of a dozen letter combinations — four of two letters, four of three letters and four of four letters. Each player is given the same list, for example:

SY	NISS	PLA
EX	AWN	POLI
IB	IEN	UPTU
JU	BEC	ROVO

They then have 10 minutes to build the longest words possible containing those letters, excluding plurals. But the combinations must appear within the words, not at the beginning or end. Thus, from the above list, answers such as POLITICIAN OR EXTRAORDINARY would be ruled out. When the time limit is up, the players read out their words, calculating their totals by adding up the letters in each acceptable word. If a word features the required combination twice (such as STOMACHACHE for CH), the points score for that word is

doubled. The player with the highest total is declared the resident brain-box and will probably be shunned for the remainder of the evening.

Answers for the above list could be:

MONOSYLLABIC	12
DEXTERITY	9
FLIBBERTIGIBBET	30
PREJUDICIAL	11
RECOGNISED	10
MULLIGATAWNY	12
COMEDIENNE	10
BARBECUED	9
ESPLANADE	9
TRAMPOLINE	10
VOLUPTUOUS	10
PROVOCATIVE	11
TOTAL	143

Similes

Players: Any number

You will need:

A variety of small objects, pieces of card

Think up a list of everyday objects that are used in similes ('as bright as a button', 'as neat as a new pin' etc) and places these articles on a table on a series of numbered cards. Players have to write down the simile suggested by each object. Other items which could come in handy for this game include a beetroot ('as red as a beetroot'), the ace of spades ('as black as the ace of spades'), a wine glass ('as clear as crystal'), a whistle ('as clean as a whistle'), two pieces of wood ('as thick as two short planks') and a table tennis bat ('as blind as a bat'). You may have problems finding a newt to put on the table but by the end of the party that could be the most apt comparison of all.

Desert Islanders

Players: 5-10

Armed with pencil and paper, players are asked to write down the six items which they would take with them to a desert island, and why. The answers should be as truthful as possible although any husband who names 'the blonde next door' is liable to receive a few dirty looks from his wife. There are no winners, as such, to this game although a prize could be awarded for the most amusing list.

Celebrity Desert Islanders

Players: 5-10

In this less traumatic adaptation of 'Desert Islanders', players have to write down a list of six items which a well-known personality might choose to take to a desert island. Each player is handed a card bearing the name of a different famous person, dead or alive, true or fictional, anyone from Ethelred the Unready to Deputy Dawg. This game is excellent therapy for exorcising pet hates. For example you might decide that Chris Evans should do a great public service by taking with him to a desert island Shane Richie, Noel Edmonds, Freddie Starr, Ruth from EastEnders, Emlyn Hughes and The Fugees.

Pseudonyms

Players: Any number

Flick through the books on your shelves to compile a list of 20 people who were born with a different name to that with which they eventually found fame. Hand a copy of the list to each player and give them 10 minutes to come up with as many correct identifications as possible. The following are worthy stand-bys in case you get stuck:

Archibald Leach (Cary Grant)
Frances Gumm (Judy Garland)
Diana Fluck (Diana Dors)
Charles Lutwidge Dodgson (Lewis Carroll)
Karol Wojtyla (Pope John Paul II)
Stuart Goddard (Adam Ant)
Mary Anne Evans (George Eliot)
Ruby Stevens (Barbara Stanwyck)
Sandra Goodrich (Sandie Shaw)
Jean François Marie Arouet (Voltaire)
Lewis Winogradsky (Lord Grade)
George Panos (George Michael)
Vladimir Ilyich Ulyanov (Lenin)
Marion Morrison (John Wayne)
Michael Barrett (Shakin' Stevens)
Israel Balin (Irving Berlin)
Issur Danielovitch Demsky (Kirk Douglas)
Paul Raven (Gary Glitter)
Helen Porter Mitchell (Dame Nellie Melba)
James Lablanche Stewart (Stewart Granger)

Potted Proverbs

Players: Any number

Each player is given a piece of paper with a potted proverb written on it — that is, a proverb minus all its vowels with the consonants joined together. After 30 seconds, the host calls out 'change' and, regardless of whether or not they have solved the riddle, the players pass their papers to the person on their left. The game continues in this way until the slips have travelled full circle and the players have worked on every proverb. A point is scored for each correct answer. The sort of proverbs which could be used are: STTCHNTMSVNN (A stitch in time saves nine), LKBFRYLP (Look before you leap) and NPPLDYKPSTHDCTRWY (An apple a day keeps the doctor away).

Alliteration

Players: Any number

This is another intellectual game whereby each player selects a letter from the alphabet and sets out to write a news item, a poem or a short story in which every word begins with his or her chosen letter. This can be tough going even for those with more than a GCSE in woodwork so it is advisable to allow 25 minutes' playing time. By then, it is a fairly safe bet that everyone will have had enough. When the results are read out, a prize can go to the author of the longest or most imaginative piece.

Abbreviations

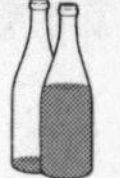

Players: Any number

Think up 20 abbreviations (some reasonably well-known, a few more obscure) and write them down on a sheet of paper. Hand a copy of the list to each player and allow them 10 minutes to work out which each set of initials stands for. If they don't know some of the answers, encourage them to make something up — their invented answers may be more appropriate than the genuine article. Who knows what a well-oiled party guest might think up for F.A.N.Y. (First Air Nursing Yeomanry)? At the end of the time limit, the player with most correct answers wins. There could also be a prize for the guest with the best made-up answer. Here are a few suggestions for abbreviations — there is usually a good list in the back of a dictionary.

A.C.A. (Associate of the Institute of Chartered Accountants)
A.S.L.E.F. (Associated Society of Locomotive Engineers & Firemen)
B.R.C.S. (British Red Cross Society)
C.B.E. (Commander of the British Empire)
E.T.A. (Estimated Time of Arrival)
F.B.I. (Federal Bureau of Investigation)
F.R.S.G.S. (Fellow of the Royal Scottish Geographical Society)
G.M.T. (Greenwich mean time)
I.C.I. (Imperial Chemical Industries)
L.C.P. (Licentiate of the College of Preceptors)
L.T.A. (Lawn Tennis Association)
M.I.C.E. (Member of the Institution of Civil Engineers)
N.A.T.O. (North Atlantic Treaty Organisation)
N.C.O. (non-commissioned officer)
R.C.M.P. (Royal Canadian Mounted Police)
R.W.S. (Royal Society of Painters in Water Colours)
S.P.E. (Society for Pure English)
T.W.A. (Trans-World Airlines)
V.H.F. (Very High Frequency)
Y.H.A. (Youth Hostels Association)

Epitaphs

Players: Any number

Dorothy Parker wanted 'Excuse my dust' put on her headstone, while W.C. Fields said that his epitaph should be: 'On the whole I'd rather be in Philadelphia.' Here, players are given the task of writing a witty epitaph either for a celebrity, or for someone else in the room. Depending on how well you know your fellow guests, it might be advisable to make the suggestions reasonably good-natured. Headstone comments such as Robert Benchley's suggested inscription for a movie star ('SHE SLEEPS ALONE — AT LAST') may not go down too well in certain company...

Word Search

Players: Any number

Draw up a list of a dozen distinctive word features and give the players two minutes to come up with one example of each.
Here are some suggested categories:

Words ending in 'x' (onyx)
Words containing three 'e's (telephone)
Words ending in 'ic' (traffic)
Words of more than four syllables (encyclopedia)
Words beginning with 'ven' (ventriloquist)
Words containing three 'a's (aardvark)
Words with a 'q' in the middle (pique)
Words ending in 'sm' (prism)
Words beginning with 'mic' (microphone)
Words containing three 'i's (imagination)
Words of more than 14 letters (monographically)
Words beginning with 'z' (zenith)

Drawn From Memory

Players: 4-8

You will need:
Pieces of card

Draw six simple sketches on separate pieces of card. These can be something like a square with four different patterns, a boat with two sails, a house with a driveway and car or a ball with five spots. Number the cards and allow the players to study them for a total of a minute and a half. Then ask them to draw each sketch to the best of their recollection. The results will show just how much attention they were paying to detail. Award a prize to the most accurate set of reproductions.

Mad Libs

Players: 4-8

Write a short story about the people at your party, or a nursery rhyme or fable and then remove key nouns, verbs, adjectives, adverbs and people's names. For these are to be filled in by the players who have absolutely no idea what the text is about. Give each player a pencil and paper and simply call out 'adjective', 'noun', 'exclamation' or whatever. At the end of the piece, collect the various answers and read them out, inserting the players' chosen words in the spaces in your text. The results can be somewhat illuminating. For example your story could be:

THE GIRL OF MY DREAMS
'The girl of my dreams has ADJECTIVE blonde hair and ADJECTIVE eyes which remind me of PLURAL NOUN. Her skin is as smooth as a (an) ADJECTIVE NOUN and is scented like PLURAL NOUN. Her legs are shaped like a NOUN and she looks really sexy when she's wearing her ADJECTIVE NOUN. In fact I think she's got a figure like NAME OF MAN IN ROOM. When I look into her PLURAL NOUN, I

want to say, "I would really like to VERB you one day." I would ADVERB give up all my PLURAL NOUN for one night with this ADJECTIVE girl. Her name is NAME OF GIRL IN ROOM.'

This may end up as:

'The girl of my dreams has mouldy blonde hair and hideous eyes which remind me of dried prunes. Her skin is as smooth as a geriatric camel and is scented like Brussel sprouts. Her legs are shaped like a grand piano and she look really sexy when she's wearing her grey gas-mask. In fact I think she's got a figure like Mr. Appleby the butcher. When I look into her nail clippers, I want to say, "I would really like to garrote you one day." I would miserably give up all my pork scratchings for one night with this lice-infested girl. Her name is Mrs. Ollerenshaw.'

Or alternatively you could try:

THE WEDDING

'The wedding took place yesterday of the ADJECTIVE NAME OF MALE CELEBRITY and the ADJECTIVE FEMALE CELEBRITY. The bride's dress was made of NOUN and had a ADJECTIVE neckline. On her head she wore a NOUN. She looked quite ADJECTIVE. When the groom slipped the NOUN on her PART OF BODY, there wasn't a dry NOUN in the house. Later at the reception the bride's mother, a ADJECTIVE woman, wiped away a NOUN and said, "This is the most ADJECTIVE day of my life." With that the ADJECTIVE couple cut the NOUN with a NAME OF CUTTING IMPLEMENT. Among the presents they received were a NOUN, a NOUN and the world's largest collection of PLURAL NOUN. 'They will look lovely on our NOUN," said the bride. After the reception they set off by MEANS OF TRANSPORT for a ADJECTIVE honeymoon in PLACE.'

This could produce:

'The wedding took place yesterday of the turbo-charged Murray Walker and the repulsive Imelda Marcos. The bride's dress was made of tin and had a crude neckline. On her head she wore a potty. She looked quite ghastly. When the groom slipped the axe on her neck, there wasn't a dry toilet seat in the house. Later at the reception the bride's mother, a vindictive woman, wiped away a moth and said, "This is the most excruciating day of my life." With that the argumentative couple cut the vicar with a scythe. Among the presents they received were a rusty frying-pan, a cotton bud and the world's largest collection of moose droppings. "They will look lovely on our dinner plate," said the bride. After the reception they set off by donkey for a nauseating honeymoon in Castleford.'

Eye Test

Players: Any even number

This is a game that could get you into big trouble with your partner. Participants are divided into sexes and each man is instructed to talk to any one woman for a minute. When the time is up, the women are sent from the room and each man has to write down a description of what the woman he was talking to was wearing. The most detailed and accurate description wins. But beware. It may not always be wise to eulogise about the length (or lack of it) of a girl's skirt or the tightness of her jeans if the person in question is not your partner. The roles are then reversed with the women talking to the men for a minute before noting down in as much detail as possible what the man they were talking to said. Similarly if it was a chat-up line, it might be best to draw a discreet veil over the conversation. Whoever devised this game obviously believes that women have nothing worthwhile to say and men never wear anything worth mentioning. The only drawback is that after a few pints, most men can't remember what they've just been talking about either so when playing this game they are advised to stick to a prepared text about their job or whatever. Besides, what woman could resist an opening gambit of 'I'm in sewage'?

What's the Link?

Players: Any number

Think up a list of 20 pairs of famous people who have a common link. For instance with Robert the Bruce and Miss Muffet, the link would be spiders. Give each player a copy of the list and allow them 10 minutes to fill in the missing links between the various pairs. The one with most correct answers wins the game. Here are some possible examples:

1. William Tell and Sir Isaac Newton
2. Tab Hunter and Donny Osmond
3. Jeremy Brett and Douglas Wilmer

4. Jim Bowen and Schubert
5. Henry VIII and E.M. Forster
6. Dave Webb and Andy Linighan
7. Edward Heath and Sir Francis Chichester
8. Mrs. Arthur Daley and Maris Crane from *Frasier*
9. John Cleese and Jeffrey Archer
10. Ben Turpin and Ken Dodd
11. Henry I of England and King John
12. Norman Tebbit and Tony Hancock
13. Wolf and Zodiac
14. Ann Packer and Mary Peters
15. Mick Jagger and Bing Crosby
16. Peter Adamson and Peter Baldwin
17. James A. Garfield and William McKinley
18. Annie Lennox and Jocky Wilson
19. Billy Bunter and Frank Spencer
20. John Lennon and Jackie Wilson

Answers: 1. Apples. William Tell is supposed to have fired his crossbow at an apple on his son's head while Sir Isaac Newton is said to have started thinking about the laws of gravity after seeing an apple fall in an orchard. 2. Both had number one hits with the song 'Young Love'. 3. Both played Sherlock Holmes on television. 4. Both once worked as school teachers. 5. The fifth of Henry VIII's wives was Catherine Howard who was executed; *Howard's End* is a novel by E.M. Forster. 6. Both scored the winning goals in FA Cup final replays, Webb for Chelsea against Leeds United in 1970 and Linighan for Arsenal against Sheffield Wednesday in 1993. 7. Sailing. Both were keen sailors. 8. Neither TV characters have ever been seen. 9. Both were raised in Weston-Super-Mare. 10. Insurance. Boss-eyed silent film star Ben Turpin was insured for $100,000 against the possibility of his eyes ever becoming normal again and similarly Ken Dodd insured his distinctive teeth, the result of a schoolboy cycling accident, for over £10,000. 11. Food. Both died from over-eating. Henry perished from a surfeit of lampreys (small eel-like creatures) and John died after devouring a quantity of peaches and cider. 12. They both once had jobs as assistants in menswear shops. 13. Both appear on the TV show *Gladiators*. 14. Both won Olympic track and field gold medals for Britain, Ann Packer in the 800 metres in 1964 and Mary Peters in the pentathlon in 1972. 15. Both sang hit duets with David Bowie. Crosby and Bowie reached number three in the UK charts with 'Little Drummer Boy' in 1982 and Jagger and Bowie got to number one in 1985 with 'Dancing in the Street'. 16. Both were killed off in *Coronation Street* — Adamson as Len Fairclough, Baldwin as Derek Wilton. 17. Both

were U.S. Presidents who were assassinated in office. 18. Fish. Singer Annie Lennox and darts player Jocky Wilson both used to work in Scottish fish factories. 19. Michael Crawford, who played Frank Spencer, was one of the boys in the TV version of *Billy Bunter* in the 1950s. 20. Both had posthumous number one hits.

Which Town?

Players: 5-10

This game is a picture version of 'Charades'. The host — or a particularly artistic guest — draws a series of quick sketches, each depicting the name of a town. The other players have to study the drawings and work out the names of the towns. Popular ideas include:

A drawing of an off-licence (STOCKPORT)
A grave digger at work (BURY)
A plate-full of food (NUNEATON)
A bank robber demanding money (ANDOVER)
A man walking towards a very low bridge (MINEHEAD)

The numbers 2,4,8,16,32 (DUBLIN)
LITTLEHAMPTON should be avoided at all costs...

Pictorial Proverbs

Players: Any even number up to 12

This 'Picture Charades' game involves players doing drawings which portray well-known proverbs such as 'Make hay while the sun shines', 'A bird in the hand is worth two in the bush' and 'A nod is as good as a wink to a blind horse.' It is best played as a team game with a player from each team being told which proverb to illustrate by the host. They return to their respective groups and, without speaking or writing any words, perform their mime via a drawing. The first team to guess correctly wins the round, the game

continuing until every player has had a stint as the artist. The game can also be played with films, TV programmes and book titles.

Headlines

Players: 4-10

Have you ever wondered how *The Sun* would have reported the Battle of Hastings or how *The Mirror* would have covered the Roman invasion of Britain? Well here is your chance to find out. The host prepares a list of historical events and asks the players to think up tabloid headlines to fit them. This is probably best played as a non-competitive game with players having as many goes as they wish since some will prove more adept at this task than others. Here are a few suggestions but no doubt you can do much better:

IT'S ONE IN THE EYE FOR HAROLD
— WILY WILLY SHOOTS 'EM DOWN (Battle of Hastings)
NELSON IN DEATH-BED SNOG SCANDAL (Battle of Trafalgar)
M.P. KILLED AT RAILWAY OPENING
— DIDN'T EXPECT TRAIN TO BE ON TIME (Death of William Huskisson)

Catchphrases

Players: Any number

Think up a list of a dozen catchphrases used by famous people and characters past or present and jumble them up. The players have to pair the right person with the right catchphrase. These may prove helpful:

'Let's meet the eight who are going to generate' (Bruce Forsyth)
'Don't embawass me' (Lenny the Lion)
'You've never had it so good' (Harold Macmillan)
'Awight?" (Michael Barrymore)
'Yabba Dabba Doo' (Fred Flintstone)
'Book 'em, Danno' (Steve McGarrett)

'Heavens to Murgatroyd' (Snagglepuss)
'Yus, m'lady' (Parker)
'Just the facts, ma'am' (Sergeant Joe Friday)
'Who loves ya, baby?' (Theo Kojak)
'Before your very eyes' (Arthur Askey)
'You lucky people' (Tommy Trinder)

A Question of Taste

Players: Any number

You will need:
Blindfolds, plastic cups, assorted liquids

This game is probably more enjoyable played when the guests have warmed up a bit — in other words, had a few drinks — because it tests their sense of taste. A series of plastic cups are filled with different drinkable liquids — including washing-up liquid may seem like a fun idea at the time but might not make you terribly popular. The players are blindfolded and take it in turns to sniff and sip the liquids, writing down their guesses as to the contents as they move along the line. You want to select as great a variety of liquids as possible while slipping in a couple of closely-related wines (say a Chardonnay and a Sauvignon Blanc) to test the connoisseurs. An ideal line-up might comprise: Bovril, Marmite, Ovaltine, grapefruit juice, pineapple juice, cocoa, drinking chocolate, Bisto gravy, tap water, bottled spring water, Chardonnay and Sauvignon Blanc. The winner is either the one with most correct answers or the last to throw up.

Beheaded

Players: Any number

Each player has 10 minutes to go through the alphabet listing a word beginning with each letter which, when the first letter is removed, still makes a proper word. For example if your first word is 'ago', after deleting the 'a' you still have the word 'go'. Other examples are 'broom' ('room'), 'crook' ('rook'), 'drake' ('rake'), 'eastern' ('astern') and ending in 'yearn' ('earn') and 'zany' ('any').

The Numbers Game

Players: Any number

Prepare a list of phrases, sayings, song titles, movie titles etc, each containing a number. Copy the list and give the players a minute to fill in the appropriate numbers. For example:

The Magnificent——— (7)
The —— Steps (39)
—— Red Balloons (99)
————— Deadly Sins (7)
——— Steps to Heaven (3)
—— Trombones (76)
——-Way Stretch (2)
The ——— o'Clock Club (9)
Pebble Mill at ——(1)
—————— Days a Week (8)
Space ——— (1999)
——— And All That (1066)
————— Love Songs and You (1,000,000)

Alpha

Players: Any number

Players are given 10 minutes to list as many words as they can which begin and end with the same letter of the alphabet. The winner is the player who comes up with the longest list. Examples include: Amnesia, Dressed, Endive, Fluff, Gyrating, Hitch, Kayak, Maximum, Success, Tournament and Xerox. An alternative version is to go through the alphabet trying to think up the longest possible words beginning and ending with the same letter. A point is scored for each letter. Thus 'Partnership' scores 11 points, 'Deteriorated' 12 and 'Yellowy' 7. Problems arise when it comes to I, J, Q, U,V and Z.

The Lady's Handbag

Players: Any number

This rather quaint game invites players to enter the secret world of a lady's handbag, the contents of which have hitherto remained something of a mystery to most men. Draw up a list of items likely to be found in a lady's handbag and jumble them up into anagrams. Writing each anagram on a slip of paper, scatter the slips around the house and ask the players to unravel as many objects as they can in the space of 10 minutes. The player who has unscrambled the most answers wins the eyeshadow of his or her choice. In case you have no knowledge whatsoever of a lady's handbag, here are a few items which you might encounter with its walls: lipstick, mascara, cheque-book, comb, nail file, scissors, aspirin, door keys, purse, handkerchief, diary, perfume and, for American guests, a revolver.

Re-writing History

Players: 6 or more

Don't be put off by the title. This isn't a game solely for eminent historians — indeed they would probably frown at the frivolity of it all. Players are divided into teams, each containing three or four players, and take it in turns to suggest eight historical characters. The teams are then given 15 minutes to think up a story — the more ludicrous the better — in which all eight characters feature. At the end, the efforts are read out and the most inventive tale is named the winner. Obviously the more diverse the characters the greater scope there is for imagination. These two lists feature a good assortment through the ages:

Vlad the Impaler	Queen Victoria
Margaret Thatcher	Nell Gwynn
Edward the Confessor	Ivan the Terrible
Hitler	Boadiccea
Guy Fawkes	Ronald Reagan
Marie Antionette	Richard III
Richard Nixon	King Canute
Elizabeth I	Alfred the Great

Limericks

Players: Any number

This ever-popular pastime can be played in two ways as a party game. Either each player selects a town from an atlas and composes the entire limerick, or it becomes a group effort. In the second instance, the first player writes the first two lines and then folds the paper over concealing what he or she has written. The last word — the rhyming word — is then written in a visible place on the paper. The second player writes the next two lines before handing over to the third player who composes the last line, making sure that it rhymes with the word at the top of the sheet. A prize goes to the wittiest offering. In the unlikely event that you are unsure of the style of limericks, here is an example which has the added advantage of promoting dental hygiene:

'There was a young lady from Neath
Who had the most God-awful teeth
Those that weren't blacked
Were decidedly cracked
With lorry-loads of plaque underneath.'

Clearly anyone who has the misfortune to pluck Llanfairpwllgwyngyllgogerychwyrndrobwllllantysiliogogogoch from the atlas is in for a tough time.

Picture Puzzle

Players: 5-10

You will need:
Magazines or travel brochures

Look through some old magazines or travel brochures and find a series of large photographs (one per player) with plenty of detail. Then choose a letter from the alphabet — something easy like S, C or T — and ask each player to write down as many things as they can see beginning with that letter in their photograph. At the end of two minutes, get them to read out their answers. To ensure fair play, players should draw on their picture a circle around each item they list. That way the judge can determine whether that white spot is really a distant seagull or just a print mark.

First Name Terms

Players: Any number

The host dictates to the players a list of 20 surnames of famous people, dead or alive, true or fictional, and gives them two minutes in which to write down the appropriate first name. In order to make the game more competitive, it is a good idea to include a few surnames which could have more than one Christian name — for instance 'Rutherford' could refer to Ernest or Margaret. Here, players get one point for a correct name which is also on other people's lists of answers, but two points for a name which nobody else has thought of. This list might help to get you started:

1. Hemingway
2. Gardner
3. Rameau
4. Edison
5. Doggie
6. Copernicus
7. Becker
8. Joyce
9. Marples
10. Fox
11. Hobbs
12. Madgwick
13. Schumacher
14. Watts
15. Tyler
16. Rendell
17. Poulsen
18. Crompton
19. Fontana
20. Wainthropp

Answers: 1. Ernest 2. Ava, Erle Stanley or John 3. Jean-Philippe 4. Thomas Alva 5. Auggie 6. Nicolaus 7. Boris or Lydia 8. James or William 9. Ernest 10. Edward, James, Samantha, Noosha, Charles or George 11. Thomas or Jack 12. Abel 13. Michael or Ralf 14. Alan, George, Charlie, David or Curly 15. Wat, John or Bonnie 16. Ruth 17. Valdemar 18. Richmal or Samuel 19. Domenico, Lucio or Wayne 20. Hetty

Crazy Definitions

Players: Any number

The art of punning has never received the credit it deserves. It is always looked down upon by supposedly superior wits — indeed the punmaster is treated with the sort of disdain usually reserved for double-glazing salesmen. But here is a game where such wordsmiths can come into their own, concocting preposterous definitions for everyday words. Each player is assigned a letter of the alphabet and has 10 minutes to come up with as many daft definitions as possible for words beginning with that letter. The one with most answers is the winner. These excruciating examples will help set the tone:

Festival — in the beginning
Fungi — man who likes to party
Parasite — army camp
Disgruntled — a pig that has lost its voice
Nickname — steal someone else's identity
Battery — place where bats live
Minimum — a small parent

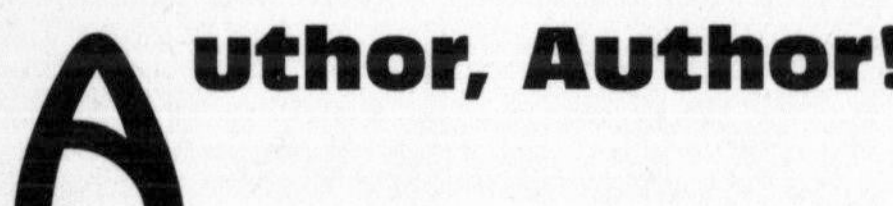

Author, Author!

Players: Any number

Another punning game. Players are given 10 minutes to think up as many authors as possible with punning names to fit book titles, such as the old schoolboy favourite *My Life of Crime* by Robin Banks. Here are a few more:

The Medical Guide by Arthur Itis
A Life of Prosecution by Bill Stickers
Word Games by Anna Gram
Lewis Carroll: a Biography by Alison Wonderland
An Introduction to Gay Sex by William Fitzpatrick
The Works of Rossini by Barbara Seville
Depression for Beginners by Mona Lott
Oh Yes He Did! by Betty Never

Acrostics

Players: Any number

Choose a word of six or seven letters from a newspaper and get the players to write the word down in a column on the left side of their paper and then to write the same word in reverse, i.e. upwards, on the right-hand side. If the chosen word is MENTHOL, the sheet would look like this:

M	L
E	0
N	H
T	T
H	N
O	E
L	M

The players then have five minutes to write the longest words they can think of beginning and ending with the letters marked out by the columns. A point is scored for each letter. Here is how it works:

MinstreL	= 8
EgO	= 3
NintH	= 5
TransparenT	=11
HistoriaN	= 9
OperatE	= 7
LogarithM	= 9

Total: 52

Young at Heart

Players: Any number

If you're a fan of old children's TV programmes like *Trumpton*, *The Clangers* and *Thunderbirds*, then this is the game for you. Kids' favourites have habitually operated in twos — all you have to do is think up a list of characters and their sidekicks, jumble them around and get the players to pair them up again correctly. Be prepared for plenty of angst as the local building society manager desperately tries to think of the name of Yogi Bear's partner. To put him out of his misery, tell him it was Boo Boo. Here are some other suitable pairs:

The Lone Ranger and Tonto
Batman and Robin
Hawkeye and Chingachgook
The Range Rider and Dick West
Secret Squirrel and Morocco Mole
Quick Draw McGraw and Baba Looie
Ivanhoe and Gurth
Hector Heathcote and Winston
Twizzle and Footso the cat
Mike Mercury and Jimmy Gibson
Dick Dastardly and Muttley

Self-Portraits

Players: 5-10

The players are seated around a table and told to draw a self-portrait. But just as they are about to begin, the host points out that it must be done with the hand they don't normally write with. So a right-handed person will have to draw left-handed. Unless a number of the guests are ambidextrous, the end results will look like an exhibition of abstract art. A prize should go to the most gallant attempt. The least inspiring artist could be told to paint himself in oils... as long as you show him where you keep the Duckham's.

Road Signs

Players: Any number

Compile a list of around 10 road signs, but only write the first letter of each word of the command, showing the remaining letters as asterisks. Thus 'No Parking' would appear as N*P******. Hand copies of the list to the players and allow them five minutes to fill in the answers. The winner receives a free copy of the Highway Code. Here are some other suggestions:

1. K***L***
2. R*****S****N**
3. N*O*********
4. B**S***
5. H****P****C*******
6. A****O***
7. O**W**S*****
8. N*R****T***
9. G***W**
10. D***C**********A****

Answers: 1. Keep Left 2. Reduce Speed Now 3. No Overtaking 4. Bus Stop 5. Heavy Plant Crossing 6. Ahead Only 7. One Way Street 8. No Right Turn 9. Give Way 10. Dual Carriageway Ahead

Brand Names

Players: Any number

Are names like Adidas and Nike all foreign to you? Do you struggle to tell the difference between Oxo and Paxo? Well you can test your knowledge — or lack of it — with this quick-fire game in which players have a minute to write down as many product brand names as they can think of beginning with a certain letter. The host starts the ball rolling by calling out a letter. If it is C, players may scribble down Coca-Cola, Caramac, Cheddars, Clark's Shoes, Crunchie, Curly-Wurly, Cadbury's Cream Eggs, Charlie, Chanel No. 5 etc. At the end of the minute, the host calls out another letter and the players must write down as many brand names as they can think of starting with that letter. The game continues in this way until five letters have been covered and everybody's arm is about to drop off. The player with most brand names wins a bottle of Martini; the loser gets a bottle of Harpic.

Human Acronyms

Players: Any number

Each player is given the name of a famous person and told to think of an appropriate sentence in which each word begins with the letters of the celebrity's surname and in that order. Thus a sentence based on Tony Blair could read: 'Boyish Looks Accrue Instant Rewards.' The game can also be played using the names of friends although this has been known to cause offence. For instance Colin may be a friend no longer if described as 'Clumsy Oaf Lives In Norwood' while Shaun may not be too thrilled to hear himself labelled 'Surly Hypocrite And Uncouth Neighbour'.

Famous Last Words

Players: Any number

Each player is given 15 minutes to think up appropriate last words for five famous living people or, if it is not thought to be tempting fate, for five friends at the party. Maybe Bruce Forsyth's final words would be, 'It was nice to see you, to see you nice.' Or Steve Davis might gasp, 'I should never have missed that pink in 1983.' Or Arnold Schwarzenegger might vow with his dying breath, 'I'll be back.' Give your imagination full rein.

Okapi

Players: Any number

The players are given 10 minutes to think up as many five-letter words as they can in which the first letter is a vowel, the second a consonant, the third a vowel, the fourth a consonant and the last letter another vowel. An example of a word with this combination of letters is Okapi — hence the name of the game. Other words which fit into the category include: Irate, Alive, Arena, Unite, Opera, Awake, Aroma, Elope, Evade, Image, Abide and Urine. The player with the longest list wins.

Lucky Numbers

Players: Any number

Prepare a list of some 20 facts connected with numbers and write them out in abbreviated form. For instance 24 hours in a day would be written 24 = H in a D and seven days in a week would be 7 = D in a W. Give a copy of the list to each player and allow them 10 minutes to fill in the answers. These may prove useful:

1. 360 = D in a C
2. 18 = F-C C C
3. 9 = I in the C I
4. 57 = H V
5. 6 = S to a H
6. 51 = S in A
7. 7 = W of the A W
8. 12 = P in a W L T
9. 16 = O in a P
10. 49 = N in the L
11. 8 = F in a M
12. 77 = S S
13. 52 = P C in a P
14. 5 = G L
15. 29 = D in F in a L Y
16. 64 = Y in the R of Q V
17. 18 = H on a G C
18. 4 = O in the W
19. 32 = D F at which W F
20. 13 = a B D

Answers: 1. Degrees in a Circle 2. First-Class Cricket Counties 3. Islands in the Channel Islands 4. Heinz Varieties 5. Sides to a Hexagon 6. States in America 7. Wonders of the Ancient World 8. Players in a Women's Lacrosse Team 9. Ounces in a Pound 10. Numbers in the Lottery 11. Furlongs in a Mile 12. Sunset Strip 13. Playing Cards in a Pack 14. Great Lakes 15. Days in February in a Leap Year 16. Years in the Reign of Queen Victoria 17. Holes on a Golf Course 18. Oceans in the World 19. Degrees Fahrenheit at which Water Freezes 20. A Baker's Dozen

Linkwords

Players: Any number

More work for the long-suffering host! Think up a series of a dozen or so linkwords — words which can be linked to a word before or after. An example is Sheep (Dog) Biscuit. Here the linkword is Dog because it can connect to the word either side — Sheepdog and Dog biscuit. Having compiled your list, copy it out on sheets of paper and give the players five minutes to come up with the answers. These should help to give you the general idea:

1. Danger (Mouse) Trap
2. Greg (Norman) Tebbit
3. Nigel (Short) Bread
4. Down (Fall) Out
5. John (Major) Tom
6. Baseball (Bat) Mobile
7. Bus (Station) Wagon
8. Boy (George) Bush
9. Old (Spice) Girls
10. Rocking (Horse) Box
11. Sand (Paper) Chain
12. Clive (James) Last

Powders

Players: 5-10

You will need:
Various edible powders or granules, saucers

This is another tasting game but here, instead of liquids, players have to identify a succession of powders — no illegal substances please! The powders are arranged in a row of saucers and the players move along the line tasting

each one in turn by dipping in the end of a finger. They then have to write down what they think it is. Salt, flour, sugar, gravy granules and bicarbonate of soda are staple ingredients of this game.

Literary Lions

Players: Any number

In this game players write, in a variety of literary styles, on a topic which would appear eminently unsuitable. Each player writes on a slip of paper the name of a celebrated author, a newspaper or a magazine. While the slips are being collected, the host announces the topic. The slips are then mixed up and the players each draw one. Listen for the gasps of horror as players realise that they have to write an article on The Virtues of Ready-Mix Concrete in the style of Charles Dickens; or *The Sun*; or Barbara Cartland; or Shakespeare; or *Cosmopolitan*. Other suggested subjects are:
A Weekend in Cleethorpes
Flared Trousers: A Fashion Statement
Home Electrical Maintenance
An Alien Landing
The Music of Roger Whittaker

Blurbs

Players: 4-8

You will need:
Some paperback novels, a hat or bowl

This game is extremely popular amongst budding authors. The host chooses a novel from the shelves and writes down the first line on a slip of paper. It is best not to choose a book with a classic opening line, such as *Rebecca*, because it will rather defeat the object of the game. With the players

assembled, he or she then reads out the blurb on the back cover of the book, making sure that the players don't see the title, the author or any other identifying features. Having gathered that this is a tale of 'smouldering passion, insatiable greed and homicidal envy', they then have five minutes in which to compose what they think could be the first line of the novel. Their endeavours are then collected and put into a hat or bowl with the slip of paper bearing the authentic first line. The host then reads out all of the slips and the players have to guess which is the genuine article. The first person to do so wins the round and the game continues with the host reading out the blurb from another pre-selected novel. Given participants with literary leanings, it is surprising how often some of the made-up first lines sound better than the real thing.

The End Zone

Players: Any number

Think up a list of around 20 words which finish in the letters END. Then write out a clue for each one. Give a copy of the list to each player and allow them 10 minutes to come up with the answers. To save you exercising the grey matter unduly, here's one I made earlier:

1. Correct
2. Climb
3. Protect
4. Salary
5. Clergyman
6. Mix
7. Companion
8. Sell
9. Have in mind
10. Swell out
11. Hang up
12. Profess falsely
13. Go down
14. Repair
15. Dispatch
16. Make crooked

17. Take care of
18. Give warning of
19. Bestow
20. Pay out

Answers: 1. Amend 2. Ascend 3. Defend 4. Stipend 5. Reverend 6. Blend 7. Friend 8. Vend 9. Intend 10. Distend 11. Suspend 12. Pretend 13. Descend 14. Mend 15. Send 16. Bend 17. Tend 18. Portend 19. Lend 20. Spend

The Ageing Process

Players: Any number

Scour the newspapers for the 'Whose birthday today' section and prepare a list of diverse celebrities or famous people together with their ages. Having supplied the players with paper and pencil, call out your list of names and ask them to fill in what they think each celebrity's current age is. Handy hint: Most actresses are 29. After collecting up their estimates, read out the correct answers and wait for comments like: 'He was old when Methuselah was a lad!' or 'She's had more face lifts than Covent Garden!' Add up the discrepancies on each answer sheet between the proper ages and the guesses and the winner will be the player with the smallest overall difference. These ages are current at 1 November 1997:

Meryl Streep 48
Martina Navratilova 41
Nadia Comaneci 35
Prince Philip 76
Bob Dylan 56
Prince Charles 48
Vanessa Redgrave 60
Alan Bennett 63
Joanna Lumley 51
Muhammad Ali 55
Des O'Connor 65
Barbara Streisand 55
Sophia Loren 63
Pele 57
Bob Monkhouse 69

Silhouettes

Players: 5-10

You will need:
Old magazines, some plain card

Sift through a pile of old magazine and find some nice glossy photographs. Then carefully cut out certain objects from the photos — maybe a table, a knife, a bunch of flowers, a sofa — so that, when set against plain card, they leave a series of silhouettes. The players have to study the pictures and write down what they think the missing objects are. The one with the most correct answers claims the spoils.

Stud Book

Players: Any number

This is a game of intelligence and imagination which will appeal to students of the horse-racing form book. Compile a list of 20 imaginary sires and dams, the names of which are loosely connected in some way. The players then have 15 minutes to think up suitable names for the various foals. Although you will have prepared your answers in advance, there is no hard and fast rule about right or wrong. One of the players may come up with an equally good — if not better — suggestion than your own so points have to be awarded for ingenious answers as well as the ones you had thought of. The following should help you get out of the starting stalls:

1. By Ajuga out of Last Post
2. By Ian Botham out of Tar Baby
3. By Plug Away out of The Feather
4. By Spaniel out of The Artist
5. By Oak Tree out of Sirocco
6. By Lyons Maid out of Day of Rest
7. By San Francisco out of Sweet Slumbers

8. By Hawkeye out of King Edward
9. By Eros out of Trapeze Artist
10. By Cadbury's Flake out of Cinderella
11. By Pigtail out of Union
12. By Julius Caesar out of Proboscis
13. By Wentworth out of Society Dance
14. By Eiffel Tower out of First Class Mail
15. By The Pied Piper out of Grand National
16. By Cornflake out of Dr. Crippen
17. By Homburg out of Paul Daniels
18. By Yorkshire Cricketer out of Victor Kiam
19. By Mandarin out of Sir Robert
20. By Providence out of Communist

Answers: 1. Bugle 2. Cricket Pitch 3. Electric Light 4. Prince Charles 5. Woodwind 6. Ice Cream Sundae 7. California Dreaming 8. Mashed Potato 9. Piccadilly Circus 10. Chocolate Buttons 11. Ayr United 12. Roman Nose 13. Golf Ball 14. French Letter 15. Rat Race 16. Cereal Killer 17. Hat Trick 18. Close Shave 19. Orange Peel 20. Rhode Island Red

The game is open to abuse. Manchester United fans might argue that By Badly out of Contention must be Newcastle United. The game can also be played in reverse whereby players are given the names of the foals and have to think of appropriate names for the sires and dams.

Keywords

Players: Any number

A slightly easier game involving word combinations is 'Keywords'. Here the host calls out a proper three-letter word such as 'rid', and gives the players three minutes to write down as many words as possible which contain that keyword. Examples could be: arid, pride, ride, grid, griddle, riddle, bride, bridle, acrid, lurid, meridian, pride, stride and torrid.

Blockbusters

Players: 5-10

Pluck a letter from the alphabet and think up 12 questions, the answers to which are all words beginning with that letter. Read out your questions and after each one give the players 30 seconds to jot down the answer. At the end of all 12 questions, see who has managed the highest score. If the game proves popular, you can move on to another letter... or two... or three... or four... until everyone is intellectually exhausted. If your chosen letter is F, your questions could be:

1. Which F was an English comedian famed for his ukulele?
2. On what F might you find a stamen, a corolla and a calyx?
3. What F has a capital of Helsinki?
4. Which F starred in *The Prisoner of Zenda*?
5. Which F is a port in Western Australia?
6. Which F succeeded Richard Nixon as U.S. President?
7. Which F is a short raised deck at the bow of a ship?
8. Which F is equivalent to 220 yards?
9. Which F was a style of painting inspired by van Gogh?
10. Which F is a member of the thrush family?
11. Which F was an Italian mathematician who had a series of numbers named after him?
12. Which F is a Scottish football team playing at Brockville?

Answers: 1. Formby (George) 2. Flower 3. Finland 4. Fairbanks (Douglas Jr) 5. Fremantle 6. Ford (Gerald) 7. Fo'c's'le 8. Furlong 9. Fauvism 10. Fieldfare 11. Fibonacci 12. Falkirk

Twisted Tunes

Players: Any number

Prepare a list of 15 song titles and convert the words into anagrams. Give the players 15 minutes to unravel the letters. The one with the most correct titles could win a prize like a Crowded House CD, the loser getting a Nana Mouskouri CD. These may save you some time:

(To make things a little easier, the years of the songs are in brackets)

1. Llawdrowne (1995)
2. Homebani Shayprod (1975)
3. Noxeran (1979)
4. Spottyresee (1995)
5. Pungjim Ajkc Shalf (1968)
6. Gyabg Storesur (1980)
7. Tubestuist (1966)
8. Pushdad Oyu Café (1981)
9. Ttamschalk Enm dan Ttamschalk Stac dan Gods (1978)
10. Gonkwin Em Gonkwin Uoy (1977)
11. Scaleser Wipersh (1984)
12. Ramka Loncheema (1983)
13. Threes a Yug Skrow Wond Eht Hiphopsc Wrasse She Slive (1981)
14. Gribed Rove Droublet Trawe (1970)
15. Ni Het Arey 5252 (1969)

Answers 1. Wonderwall 2. Bohemian Rhapsody 3. Roxanne 4. Stereotypes 5. Jumping Jack Flash 6. Baggy Trousers 7. Substitute 8. Shaddup You Face 9. Matchstalk Men and Matchstalk Cats and Dogs 10. Knowing Me Knowing You 11. Careless Whisper 12. Karma Chameleon 13. There's a Guy Works Down The Chipshop Swears He's Elvis 14. Bridge Over Troubled Water 15. In The Year 2525

Awkward Letters

Players: Any number

This game is for people whose idea of a good read is a dictionary. Some English words boast letter combinations which are so unusual, it's difficult to envisage them occurring in any known word. An example is the WKW in awkward. So give your dictionary buffs the thrill of a lifetime by drawing up a list of a dozen or so tricky three-letter combinations and allow them 10 minutes to find English words into which the sequences fit. If anybody comes up with a word different from the one you'd thought of, award them an extra point. Here are some good examples: vacUUM, harDSHip, baZAAr, duMBFound, quaRTZ, autUMNal, laWYEr, haphAZArd, witHHOld and preSBYtery.

Who Said That?

Players: Any number

From time to time, everyone wishes they had come up with a witty riposte or a *bon mot*, especially at parties. Perhaps you and your guests can draw inspiration from the words of others as you play this game based on quotations. Search through a book of quotations (there are plenty in the library if you don't have any at home). Pick out 20 of the best, jumble up the speakers' names and give players five minutes to attribute the quotes to the correct people. This list of verbal gems may prove helpful:

1. 'There is only one thing in the world worse than being talked about, and that is not being talked about.'
2. 'He who can, does; he who cannot, teaches...'
3. 'What you said hurt me very much. I cried all the way to the bank.'
4. 'I never hated a man enough to give him his diamonds back.'
5. 'A successful man is one who makes more money than his wife can spend. A successful woman is one who can find such a man.'
6. 'Anyone who goes to a psychiatrist should have his head examined.'

7. 'I used to be Snow White, but I drifted.'
8. 'Asking a working writer what he thinks about critics is like asking a lamp-post what it thinks about dogs.'
9. 'I don't want to achieve immortality through my work. I want to achieve it through not dying.'
10. 'The reports of my death are greatly exaggerated.'
11. 'When a man fell into his anecdotage it was a sign for him to retire from the world.'
12. 'Too bad all the people who know how to run the country are busy driving taxi cabs and cutting hair.'
13. 'A woman's place is in the wrong.'
14. 'You never realise how short a month is until you pay alimony.'
15. 'A bank is a place that will lend you money if you can prove that you don't need it.'
16. 'Life is rather like a tin of sardines — we're all of us looking for the key.'
17. 'Moral Indignation is jealousy with a halo.'
18. 'A bore is a man who, when you ask him how he is, tells you.'
19. 'Gossip is the art of saying nothing in a way that leaves practically nothing unsaid.'
20. 'A cannibal is a guy who goes into a restaurant and orders the waiter.'

A. George Burns
B. Mae West
C. Bert Leston Taylor
D. James Thurber
E. Oscar Wilde
F. Mark Twain
G. Liberace
H. Walter Winchell
I. John Barrymore
J. Alan Bennett
K. Zsa Zsa Gabor
L. Sam Goldwyn
M. Bob Hope
N. John Osborne
O. George Bernard Shaw
P. Lana Turner
Q. Woody Allen
R. Jack Benny

S. Benjamin Disraeli
T. H.G. Wells
Answers: 1E 2O 3G 4K 5P 6L 7B 8N 9Q 10F 11S 12A 13D 14 I 15M 16J 17T 18C 19H 20R

Hollywood Put Downs

Players: Any number

Hollywood can be a playground of bitchiness with the movie industry's cruellest jibes being reserved for the inflated egos and wage packets of its stars. With so much wit at their disposal the comments of executives, critics and fellow performers make wonderful reading, as long as you're not on the receiving end. For this quotation game, select 10 Hollywood barbs and ask the players to write down whom they think was the object of ridicule. You can either call out the quotes or have them printed on sheets of paper. In the latter event, allow the players five minutes to come up with the answers. Here are a few to fire your imagination:

1. 'Well, at least he has finally found his true love — what a pity he can't marry himself' — Frank Sinatra
2. 'Wet she's a star, dry she ain't' — Joe Pasternak
3. 'Working with her is like being hit over the head with a Valentine card' — Christopher Plummer
4. 'To tell the honest truth, he isn't such a helluva good lay' — Carole Lombard
5. 'A professional amateur' — Laurence Olivier
6. 'She is not even an actress... only a trollop' — Gloria Swanson
7. 'I love to play bitches, and she certainly helped me in this part' — Joan Crawford
8. 'As wholesome as a bowl of cornflakes and at least as sexy' — Dwight MacDonald
9. 'She ran the gamut of emotions from A to B' — Dorothy Parker
10. 'Silicone from the knees up' — George Masters

Answers: 1. Robert Redford 2. Esther Williams 3. Julie Andrews 4. Clark Gable 5. Marilyn Monroe 6. Lana Turner 7. Norma Shearer 8. Doris Day 9. Katharine Hepburn 10. Raquel Welch

Personal Column

Number of players: 4-8

You will need:
Newspapers

Players are asked to construct a short advertisement for inclusion in the personal columns of a newspaper or magazine. You know the sort of thing: 'Sincere boy, 20, seeks girl with own house, yacht, sports car and annual income of over £150,000. No photo necessary.' But the catch to the game is that the players' choice of words is strictly limited. When you supply the pencils and paper needed to write out the advertisements, also give each player a strip from a newspaper. In size this should amount to one column from a broadsheet like *The Daily Telegraph* or *The Times* or two columns from a tabloid such as the *Daily Mail* or *Daily Express*. Apart from two 'free' words of their own choice, all of the words for each player's advertisement must be taken from their cutting. And to ensure fair play, the words selected from the newsprint must be circled. However, there are no restrictions as to the order in which the words can be used. When everybody has finished their composition — 20 minutes should be sufficient — ask the players to read out their efforts and marvel at how a tender plea for artistic companionship has emerged from a cutting about waste-disposal methods in Mongolia.

Odd One Out

Players: Any number

This is always a popular game at parties and one that is not necessarily too intellectually demanding. However, as with all quiz games, if you have a highbrow guest list, you can make the questions much harder. Prepare 10 groups of four names, covering people, places etc. In each case, three of the names will have something in common — the players' task is to find the odd one out. The winner is the one with most correct answers in 10 minutes but,

unless you want to have a mutiny on your hands, do remember to be flexible. Someone may come up with an answer which, although it is not the one on your list, may still be perfectly acceptable. In such cases, it is diplomatic not to act as sole judge but to listen to the wishes of the majority. Here are a few sample 'Odd Ones Out':

1. Copperhead, taipan, agama and fer de lance.
2. *I'm All Right, Jack*, *Dr. Strangelove*, *The Wrong Box* and *Those Magnificent Men in Their Flying Machines*.
3. Unst, Hoy, Yell and Fetlar.
4. George Swindin, Billy Wright, Peter Shreeves and Don Howe.
5. The Hollies, The Searchers, Herman's Hermits and Freddie and the Dreamers.
6. Earl of Roseberry, Marquess of Salisbury, Earl of Derby and Earl of Liverpool.
7. 17, 13, 14 and 19
8. Pink, Chrysanthemum, Sweet William and Carnation.
9. Madam, sonic, radar and noon
10. Athabasca, Saskatchewan, Peace and Green.

Answers: 1, Agama — it's a lizard, the rest are snakes 2, *Those Magnificent Men in Their Flying Machines* — the other films all featured Peter Sellers. 3, Hoy. It is one of the Orkney Islands — the other three are part of the Shetlands. 4, Peter Shreeves. He managed Tottenham Hotspur Football Club — the others managed Arsenal. 5, The Searchers. They came from Liverpool — the others hailed from Manchester. 6, Earl of Roseberry. He was a Liberal Prime Minister — the others were all Conservatives. 7, 14 — the only one which is not a prime number. 8, Chrysanthemum — the other three are members of the Dianthus family. 9,. Sonic. The remainder are palindromes — they read the same backwards as forwards. 10, Green. It is a river in the United States. The other three are in Canada.

Royal Academy

Players: 6-10

Divide the players into two teams. On the command 'Go!', one member of each team trots over to the host who gives them both the same scene to draw. They scuttle back to their groups and set to work drawing without uttering a single word, while the other team members have to guess what the illustration is supposed to be. The game can be played over a number of rounds with the host supplying a different subject and the teams a different artist for each round. The team that achieves most correct solutions is declared the winner. The more unusual the subject for illustration, the more enjoyable the game will be. Suggestions include Pope John Paul II shopping in Tesco, Batman taking a bath and Queen Victoria appearing on *Blind Date*.

Guess the Slogan

Players: Any number

Write out 20 well-known advertising slogans and give players 10 minutes to fill in the names of the products concerned. If your mind has gone blank, here are a few suitable examples:

'The Listening Bank' (Midland Bank)
'The Sweet You Can Eat Between Meals' (Milky Way)
'The Amber Nectar' (Fosters Lager)
'Pure Genius' (Guinness)
'The Drive of Your Life' (Peugeot)

Collective Nouns

Players: Any number

We are blessed with some curious collective nouns, particularly in the world of ornithology. So let's hear it for a murmuration of starlings, a parliament of owls and an ostentation of peacocks, not to mention an exaltation of larks. A challenging game is for players to try and invent their own highly appropriate collective nouns. For instance, the collective noun for probate solicitors could be a clash of wills or a gathering of sperm donors might be a packet of seeds. Give everyone 10 minutes to indulge in this pastime while you're replenishing the drinks and then read out their creations. After such mental exertion, the least you can do is award a prize to the wittiest submission.

Talent Spotter

Players: Any number

See how good your guests are at spotting celebrities by cutting a dozen or so photographs from magazines or colour supplements, sticking them on paper and giving the players five minutes to name as many as they can. Don't choose people who are too well-known or too obscure (the Queen is a bit of a giveaway while virtually any member of the Conservative shadow cabinet is impossible) but opt for B-list celebrities like Patsy Kensit, Caron Keating or Eamonn Holmes. An alternative version is to collect magazine photographs of famous faces and cut out a nose here, the eyes there, one of the chins and so on and then ask the players to make their identifications from what's left.

ATHLETIC PURSUITS

Are You There, Moriarty?

Players: Two plus onlookers

You will need:
Rolled-up newspapers, blindfolds

This is definitely not a game for those of a nervous disposition. It takes its name from Sherlock Holmes' notorious adversary, Professor Moriarty, and purports to re-enact their life and death struggle at the Reichenbach Falls. However, there is one major difference: Holmes and Moriarty did not set about each other with rolled up copies of the *Daily Star*. The contest takes place between two players, but there are sure to be plenty of enthusiastic spectators egging them on from the sidelines. Both participants are blindfolded and told to lie face-down on the floor, each grasping the other's left wrist with their left hand and clutching a rolled-up newspaper in their right hand. One then asks, 'Are you there, Moriarty?' to which the other replies, 'Yes', before quickly slithering away to another spot as the rolled-up newspaper comes crashing down from on high. If the newspaper scores a clean blow on the opponent's head, the game is won; if the strike misses, it is the other player's turn to ask the question and take aim. As each battle ends, there should be no shortage of spectators only too willing to fill the breach. After all, a lightly-throbbing head is a small price to pay for such enjoyment.

The Jaffa Relay

Players: Any even number

You will need:
Oranges

What better way of running off that fourth sausage roll, than by waddling up and down the lounge as fast as you can with an orange wedged between the head of you and your partner? Although yet to acquire Olympic status (surely this is just an oversight by the IOC), 'The Jaffa Relay' is a long-standing party favourite. Players are split into two teams and then sub-divided into pairs. Bearing in mind that the orange has to be held between the foreheads, it is advisable that those paired off are of similar height. Pairing off a six-foot lad with a girl barely five-foot in her heels is a recipe for disaster... and sore necks in the morning! The game starts with the first pairs from each team poised behind the starting line, facing each other with the orange held between their foreheads. When the starter shouts 'Go!', they set off for a line five yards away, then turn for home where their places are taken by the next pair in the team. If the orange is dropped at any time, the players must stop and replace it between their foreheads before carrying on with the race. They must not use their hands to hold the fruit in place although they can put it in position manually when handing over to their team mates. The relay continues until one team finishes. In case of accidents with exceptionally squashy oranges, it's a good idea to have a couple of spares on standby.

Treasure Hunt

Players: Any number

You will need:
An assortment of small items, pencils and paper

'Treasure Hunt' is the classic party game for enabling guests to stretch their legs in a few minutes' gentle exercise. Before the party you need to scour cupboards, the larder, even, if you are particularly brave, your teenage son's bedroom, and produce a dozen or more small items that can be secreted somewhere about the house. These could include a shoe lace, a bus ticket, a clothes peg, a pencil sharpener, a sock, a small screwdriver, a comb, a nail file, a stamp, a cork, a milk bottle top and a key. Once you have your items, it is time to hide them in suitable places. Whilst you don't want the players to find them immediately, each object must be visible — it is unreasonable to expect even Poirot to find a paper clip which has been stuffed beneath a pile of magazines. Underneath shelves or mantelpieces are always good locations, in which case you will probably need some sticky tape to make sure the item doesn't drop off. And don't hide objects in places which are too inaccessible, especially if your guests are elderly or somewhat on the rotund side. There is nothing more embarrassing than having to call out the fire brigade because one of your guests has become wedged between the fireplace and the wall while searching for that elusive milk bottle top in 'Treasure Hunt'. As you find a home for each item, don't forget to make a note of where it is — it is really frustrating if at the end of the game nobody, not even the host, has a clue where the bus ticket is. At the start of the game, call out the list of items and, having given the players pencils and paper, tell them that they have to write down each location alongside the relevant item. A tip for players is not to get too excited when discovering an object. Frantic jumping up and down, punching the air in celebration and cries of 'Eureka!' merely tend to alert your fellow competitors — far better to move away from the object and then note its location down quietly. The first player to find every item on the list wins the game or, alternatively, a limit of 20 minutes can be imposed — the one with the most correct answers in that time being declared the victor. Of course, if all of your guests happen to be myopic, you may need larger objects — a gas cooker for example. Better still, you could try playing a different game.

Apple Ducking

Players: Any number

You will need:
Tubs of water, apples (one per player)

This is another old favourite — the sort of revelry which one can imagine being played at the court of Henry VIII. The rules are simple. One or more tubs of water are placed on the floor and floating on the surface are several nice, juicy apples. Unless you are playing this game in the kitchen, it is wise to protect your carpet with some form of plastic covering. The players then have to kneel down and, without using their hands to steady the fruit, sink their heads into the water, bite into one of the bobbing apples and lift it clear. If two players are competing at the same time (this is only possible if you have a large tub), the first to emerge with an apple in his or her mouth is the winner. If players are competing individually, the contest could be decided on the basis of the fastest time. Anybody with loose dentures is advised to give this game a miss. To make the contest even more challenging, try blindfolding the players. Or you could try filling the tub with beer instead of water, the only problem being that certain guests will spend an inordinately long time below the surface an end up forgetting about the apples altogether.

Fox and Geese

Players: Any number

This game is energetic to the point of rowdiness and is therefore much loved by rugby players. It can be played either in a large room or out in the garden. One person is selected to be the mother goose and another, usually a man, to be the fox. The remainder of the players parade behind the mother goose and pretend to be little fluffy goslings, putting their arms around each other's waists to form a line. Obeying his instincts, the fox sets out to snatch as many goslings as possible but this act of carnage can only be done from the back of the line. In order to get to the back, the fox must use speed and cunning to evade the mother goose — he is not allowed to use physical force to push her out of the way. Once captured, each gosling is taken to one side (probably in preparation for the Paxo) and the ever-hungry fox tries to snatch another offspring. The more successful he gets, the harder his task becomes for it is much more difficult to avoid the mother's beak when the line behind her is short. This game is not suitable for vegans.

Kangaroo Racing

Players: Any number

You will need:
Balloons

Not a game for the faint hearted, 'Kangaroo Racing' is just one of a 101 silly things to do with balloons. Players line up at the start, each with a balloon between the knees, and on the command 'Go!', bound off down the course like kangaroos. Any racer who drops their balloon must reclaim it, replace it between their knees and start again from the spot where balloon and 'Skippy' parted company. A burst balloon results in instant disqualification. The winner is the first player to reach the finish with their balloon intact.

Pass the Clip

Players: Any even number

You will need:
A supply of paper clips

Players are divided into two teams which stand facing each other, about a yard apart. The members of each team stand with their wrists crossed in front of them so that they're clasping the opposite hands of the people on either side. At one end of each line is a small table on which are scattered a number of paper clips (one per team member). At the other end is another small table, this time empty. The game begins with the first player in line taking the hand of the player next to him or her and using it to pick up a paper clip. The second player passes it to the third player in similar fashion and it continues down the line until the last player, who has one hand free, deposits it on the table at the other end. Meanwhile, more paper clips have begun their journey from the top table. Players must keep their hands clasped to their team mates at all times and are not allowed to move their feet — although they may twist, bend and squirm their arms, legs and bodies where necessary. If a clip is dropped at any stage, the umpire picks it up and puts it back on the top table. The first team to transfer all its clips to the bottom table wins the game. Similar games can be played with oranges, apples or tennis balls.

Ping-Pong Puff

Players: 6-12

You will need:
Table tennis balls

This game is guaranteed to take your breath away. Played on a long table with a table tennis ball, it's just like the real thing except there's no net and instead of using bats, the players rely on sheer lung power. Players are divided into two teams who position themselves on opposite sides of the table. A table tennis ball is dropped into the middle of the table and the players have to try to blow the ball over the opposite edge which their opponents are defending. Each time they do so they score a point, the first team to reach 21 points being the winner. After each point, the ball is replaced in the centre of the table. Players must keep their hands behind their backs at all times. In a more refined version of the game, the players blow through straws to propel the ball.

Ankle Race

Players: 5-10

Excruciating embarrassment is never far away in an event which becomes increasingly unpredictable with each pint consumed. The competitors have to race bent over with a hand on each ankle. As they set off along the course as quickly as possible, they must keep hold of their ankles at all times. Any runner who lets go, albeit momentarily, or who trips and falls, must suffer the added indignity of having to return to the start and begin all over again. The first player to reach the finishing line in one piece is the winner. As even the most accomplished ankle racer can end up flat on his face at a moment's notice, it's essential to ensure that the course is cleared of all furniture...

The Penny Drops

Players: Any number

You will need:
A bucket of water, 50p and a supply of two-pence coins

This familiar activity, a favourite at summer fêtes, can serve as a welcome interlude during some of the more exhausting party games. A 50 pence piece is dropped into the bottom of a bucket of water and, from a standing position, each player attempts to drop a two-pence coin so that it comes to rest on top of the 50 pence. Whoever manages to do so experiences the additional satisfaction of winning the money.

The Great Grey-Green Greasy Limpopo

Players: Any number

As if proof were ever needed that many adults are really just big kids, just watch them enjoy playing this long-standing children's favourite. The game can either be played inside in a large room or outside in the garden. The Limpopo River is marked with string across the centre of the room, or lawn, from one side to the other, its imaginary banks being about eight feet apart. One player is then chosen for the coveted role of the crocodile, while the other players are explorers who try to run back and forth across the river without being caught. If the crocodile manages to touch any of them, they are automatically tagged and obliged to join the crocodile in the river with a view to catching passers-by. All the parts of the crocodile must be linked physically at all times, usually with hands around the waist, and at least one part of the reptile's body must remain in the water. The winner is the last person to remain uncaptured, by which time everybody will be ready for another drink... but not from the waters of the great grey-green greasy Limpopo!

Fleet Street

Players: Any number

You will need:
Old newspapers, pieces of card

Cut a dozen or so headlines from old newspapers. Each headline should be between six and nine words long and, most importantly, should be in a different typeface. If your choice is so restricted that you have to include two headlines with the same typeface, at least ensure that one is in block capitals while the other is in upper and lower case. Now cut each headline into four or five parts, leaving minor words such as 'the' or 'an' attached to the more significant ones. For example: 'CITY MAGISTRATES TO ACT ON INDECENT SHOWS' would be divided up thus: CITY/ MAGISTRATES/TO ACT ON/INDECENT/SHOWS. These sections should then be pasted on to separate pieces of card. Words from more than one headline can be fixed to the same card, but be careful not to put two words from the same headline on the same card. In front of the first word in each headline, write an identifying letter (A, B, C etc) together with the total number of words in the headline so that the players know the extent of their search. Then distribute the various pieces of card around the house. By remembering the type faces and the subject matter, players have to reassemble the headlines in full and with the words in the correct order. The one with the most correct solutions in 20 minutes wins the game.

Broom Hockey

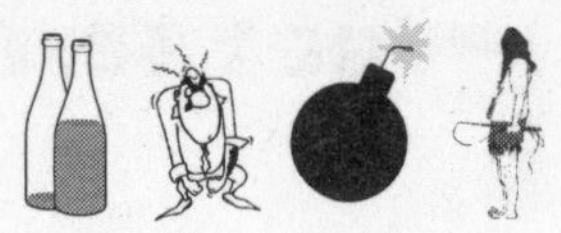

Players: 8-12

You will need:
Two brooms, a rag, four chairs

Bring all the excitement of Olympic ice hockey into your own home with this robust team game. Although shoulder padding is not essential, matters can get out of hand and happily there is every potential for the sort of mass brawl which epitomises the sport. As will be gathered from the title, the sticks in this game are brooms and the puck is an old rag. The goals are marked by two pairs of chairs at either end of the room. Players divide into two teams and stand between their goalposts, the width of the goals thus dependant on the number of players. Before the match begins, each player is given a number. If there are 10 players, they'll be numbered one to five on each team. Play starts with the host placing the rag and the two brooms in the middle of the 'rink' and then calling out number one. At that point, the two number one players rush forward, seize their brooms and begin frantically sweeping the rag towards their opponent's goal. There, the other defending team members use their feet to try to prevent the rag from being forced between the chairs, and this is where things can get a shade physical as bare ankles come into contact with solid broom handles. It has been known for defenders to stand on the broom head in a bid to immobilise the attacker. Whenever a goal is scored, the rag and brooms are returned to the centre and the next player numbers are called out. Fifteen minutes is probably quite long enough for this game, by which time a couple of your guests might already have been taken to casualty.

Cut the Tape

Players: 3-6

You will need:
Lengths of ribbon, pairs of scissors, drawing pins

Cut a roll of ribbon into roughly identical lengths, one length per player, and then pin one end of each length firmly to the wall. Arm each player with a pair of scissors and position them at the other ends of the ribbon. Their task is simply to cut their piece of ribbon into two lengths all the way along. The first to reach the end wins. Anyone who veers from a true line and accidentally cuts a piece off is disqualified. This may sound easy but it is quite a challenge, especially after a few drinks, and you have to face the very real prospect that there will be no winner, in which case you can either bestow victory upon the player who made the furthest progress or save yourself having to give anybody a prize.

Tossing the Egg

Players: 12 or over

You will need:
A supply of eggs

Unless you are either in the throes of moving or redecorating, this is definitely a game best played in the garden and preferably in old clothes. Two marker lines are laid out with string, about 10 feet apart, and the players are divided into teams of six or more people. Half the members of each team station themselves on one side of one marker line with the other half on the other side of the second marker line. The members of both halves of each team stand in single file, facing each other. Then comes the messy part. The respective team leaders are each given an egg and, on the shout of 'Go!', have to toss their egg to their waiting team mate opposite who has to catch it one-handed. Two-handed catches are strictly illegal and a broken egg results in elimination. As soon as a player tosses an egg, he or she steps out of the line to make way for his or her next team mate. The game continues in this manner until every team member has had a turn. When the team leader steps up to the marker line once more and successfully catches the egg, the game is over and that team is the winner. For a less-hazardous encounter, you could always use hard-boiled eggs.

Sardines

Players: Any number

If you need to recharge your batteries at any point in the party, what better than a quiet lie down somewhere private, particularly when it can be played within the framework of a game such as 'Sardines'? Apparently, this was once played by Queen Victoria, who may or not have been amused by the prospect of a dozen subjects secreting themselves beneath her voluminous dress. 'Sardines' is a proven favourite with all age groups. The rules are straightforward enough. One person is allowed three minutes to hide somewhere in the house, after which all of the lights are switched off and the others grope around in the dark in search of the missing player. Whenever someone finds him (or her), they have to join him in that place — be it under a bed (or in it), in the larder or even the coal cellar (the oven is not recommended, especially if it's on at the time) — whilst doing their utmost to make sure that they're not seen by any of the others. As each person discovers the hiding place, they too join the fugitives. The game continues until there's only one searcher left. Besides being an enjoyable way of filling half an hour (all the more so depending on who you're pressed up against), 'Sardines' is also an excellent way of getting rid of the party bore for a while. All you have to do is send him off to hide and then forget about him for an hour or three.

Fan the Kipper

Players: 4-8

You will need:
Newspapers and magazines, string

This deceptively violent game is another where the decks have to be cleared to allow for an obstacle-free course. Cut a page from a newspaper or magazine into the rough shape of a large kipper (you need one kipper per player) and drape lengths of string across opposite ends of the room, one acting as the start line, the other as the finish. Then give each player their kipper and a magazine, the aim being to propel one's kipper along the course by wafting the magazine behind it. Be warned, some players resort to thrashing the magazine at the floor, creating more of a hurricane than a gentle breeze giving the neighbours the distinct impression that the *Horse of the Year Show* is taking place in your lounge. There are rules governing the amount of force which can be used to speed up the kipper's progress. Kicking or molesting the aforementioned fish or prodding it with the magazine are all strictly forbidden and will result in instant disqualification, as will deliberately obstructing a fellow competitor. The winner is the first player to coerce their kipper across the finish line without cheating.

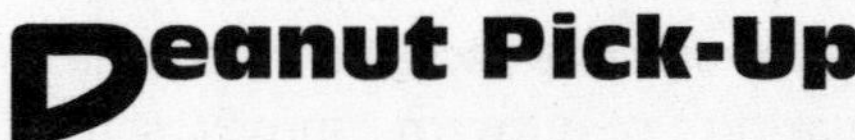

Peanut Pick-Up

Players: 5-10

You will need:
Peanuts, cocktail sticks, paper bags

This game requires concentration, composure and unerring accuracy and is therefore much more entertaining when played by people who are in the early stages of inebriation. Each player is handed two cocktail sticks and a small paper bag and is told to use the sticks to pick up the collection of peanuts which have been strewn across the floor. At some parties the host will find it necessary to scatter the peanuts on the carpet personally, at others he or she can just let events take their natural course and rely on the general untidiness of the guests. Using the cocktail sticks like chopsticks, the players crawl about the floor lifting the peanuts into the paper bag. Naturally, you are not allowed to use your hands to pick up the nuts directly. When all of the peanuts have been gathered, the player with the most bulging bag is declared the winner.

Back and Forth

Players: Any even number

You will need:

Large bowls or casserole dishes, a quantity of objects

Two teams, each with the same number of members, stand sideways in parallel lines. On the floor at one end of each team line are two large containers, such as a glass bowl, casserole dish or bucket. One of each pair of vessels is empty but the other contains a number of diverse objects — ideally there should be at least three times as many objects in each container as there are members in each team. On the command 'Go!', the first player picks an object from the vessel and passes it to the next person and so on down the line. When it reaches the far end, it begins the return journey but this time instead of players handing it to one another in front of them, it is passed behind their backs. Meanwhile, other objects will be making the outward journey, thus forcing players to switch their hands hastily from front to back. The game is over when all of one team's objects have completed both the outward and return journeys and have been deposited in the second container. The degree of difficulty can be compounded by the objects chosen. The best items are those which are tricky or particularly slippery to handle. Although the pet goldfish meets these criteria perfectly, he'll doubtless prefer it if you leave him in his bowl and use, say, a bar or wet soap instead. Other suitable objects include a hot potato, a peeled banana, a drawing pin and, depending on your circle of friends, a condom.

Identikit

Players: Any number

You will need:
Magazines or colour supplements, pieces of card, sticky tape, pencils and paper

Cut out large portrait-sized photographs of the faces of 10 famous people from magazines or colour supplements. If possible, use cover shots from the same magazine so that the paper will be of uniform texture and therefore offer fewer clues. Next, cut each photo into four sections — hair, eyes, nose and mouth — and paste or stick each one on to a separate piece of numbered card. So with 10 subjects, there will be 40 cards. Finally, place the cards in strategic positions around the house, supply the players with pencils and paper and tell them that they have 15 minutes in which to piece the faces together by writing down the correct four card numbers that bear the features of each individual celebrity. If somebody produces an identikit which turns out to have Michelle Pfeiffer's hair, Sean Bean's eyes, Anthea Turner's nose and Jimmy Hill's chin, suggest they see an optician immediately.

Name the Face

Players: Any number

You will need:
Newspapers or magazines, sticky tape, pieces of card, pencils and paper

This game also involves cutting out photographs of people from newspapers or magazines, but here it works better if the subjects aren't famous. Therefore a local paper may be your best source of material. Select around 20 photos and stick each one onto a separate piece of numbered card. Below each picture attach a slip of paper bearing a Christian name. This does not have to be the real name of the person in the photo — it can be any name you fancy. It's a good idea to choose a few similar names — Ralph and Rolf, Graham and Graeme, Anne, Anna and Annabel — just to confuse the players. Distribute the cards around the house and then give the players seven or eight minutes to try and memorise which name goes with which face. At the end of the time limit, collect the cards, remove the name slips and give each player a pencil and paper. Then hold up each card in turn and ask the players to write down the name that goes with it.

Bash the Balloon

Players: Any number

You will need:
A balloon, a blindfold, a newspaper

In this vigorous pastime, blindfolded players take it in turns to wield a rolled-up newspaper and vent their frustrations on a balloon. All of the players stand in a circle with the exception of the one whose turn it is to be blindfolded. He or she stands in the centre of the circle with rolled-up newspaper in hand. A balloon is then lobbed into the circle and, amidst cries of 'Bash the Balloon!', the player has three attempts to deliver a blow. If the balloon is hit on the first strike, three points are scored; a second-strike hit earns two points and a third-strike success one point. Bursting the balloon with any blow earns a five-point bonus — a rule which can lead to scenes of excessive violence and complaints from half the street. Failure to hit the balloon at all means no points are scored. When everyone has competed, the points are added up and the player with the highest score is the winner. In the event of a tie, there is a play-off.

Matchbox

Players: Any even number

You will need:
Matchboxes

Those who somehow manage to cram every conceivable item into their case when going on holiday — including three hairdryers, a dozen paperback novels and the microwave oven just in case the food isn't up to much — will surely relish the opportunity to take part in a packing contest on a considerably smaller scale. Players pair-off for this game, each duo being given a matchbox and orders to fill it with as many different articles as they can. They are permitted to search the house and garden but must not include more than one specimen of the same object — in other words 48 blades of grass. The winning pair are the ones who have managed to squeeze the most items into the box... as long as they've not made off with the host's jewellery.

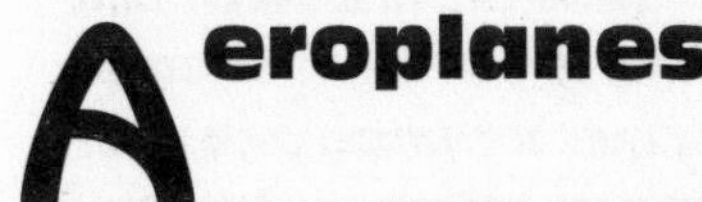

Aeroplanes

Players: Teams of 3

You will need:
Plastic or paper cups, lengths of twine

Each team of three players is issued with a 15-foot length of twine and a plastic or paper cup in the bottom of which has been cut a hole just large enough for the twine to pass through unhindered. Each team threads their length of twine through their cup. Two team members hold the ends of the twine, keeping it taut, while the third acts as blower. Before the race begins, the cup is moved along to the end of the twine which faces the open top of the cup. With all of the cups in position, the starter gets the race underway and the team blowers immediately start puffing into the open ends so as to advance their cup along the twine course as rapidly as possible. The winner is the first to reach the other end. Anyone caught smearing lubricant on his or her twine to achieve a faster passage is liable to be excluded from the next game.

Sock Fishing

Players: 6 or more

You will need:
Long socks, a variety of small objects

The object of this team game is straightforward enough — to be the first to remove a series of small items in the correct order from a man's sock, preferably one that has been washed within the last six months. Having sought out one sock per team, fill it with small objects, about a dozen in all. The range could include buttons, pebbles, beans (not baked in tomato sauce), hairpins, paper clips and coins of different sizes. To confuse the players, try and find items which feel similar. Play begins with each team leader holding a filled sock. The host calls out the first object to be found and the first players on each team rummage in the sock. They are only allowed to pull out one item at a time. If it's the right one, they take it to the host; if they are wrong they must try again. When the first object has been handed in, the host calls out the second article and the next player goes for a lucky dip. The game continues like this until the last item has been successfully located.

Kick the Can

Players: 6 or more

You will need:
A biscuit tin or can

This hectic game is best played in the garden, although a large room cleared of furniture would also suffice. A biscuit tin or a can is placed in the middle of the lawn (or room) and one player is elected to guard it. Given the physical nature of this game, it is best if that person is muscular, fearless and rugged. Or you could choose a man. It is the guard's job to prevent any of the other players from kicking the tin by touching them in a tag-like fashion. Anyone tagged is temporarily eliminated and must stand by the tin. But when another player manages to force his or her way past the guard to kick the tin, all captured players are immediately released. The game continues in this vein until either everyone has been captured or sheer exhaustion has set in. If there are more than eight players, two guards are chosen to protect the tin.

Potato Race

Players: 5-10

You will need:
Potatoes, bowls, table knives, chairs

Place up to five chairs facing inwards at either end of the room. On each of the chairs at one end, put three large potatoes and on each of the opposite chairs place a bowl. Each player is assigned a chair with the potatoes and a table knife and, on the command 'Go!', must pick up a potato on the flat end of the knife and carry it across to the bowl on the other side of the room. If a potato falls to the floor en route, it must be picked up with the knife. No hands are allowed to touch the potatoes once the race is under way The first player to deposit all three potatoes in the bowl is the winner. To accommodate more players, potato racing can be staged over two heats and a final, the fastest two from each heat going through to the eliminator. If you're contemplating buying a new carpet, you can play this game with eggs.

Scavenger Hunt

Players: 10 or more

You will need:
Pencils and paper

Short of calling a fire drill, there is no easier way of getting your guests out of the house for half an hour than by staging a 'Scavenger Hunt'. Before the party, you need to come up with a list of 20 or so articles — the more unusual the better — which can be found in your house, garden or immediate environs. You must be specific in your descriptions so that there is no room for misconception. It is not enough to say a leaf, for example, you must say an oak leaf. The players are divided into teams and each is given a list of the items to be found. They are then given 30 minutes to bring back as many things on the list as possible, the usual tactic being for the teams to split up and search for individual items. The sort of things you could include are: a blonde hair, a photograph of your family, a Boyzone poster, a book about Genghis Khan, a garden gnome, a bra, a Peter Rabbit alarm clock, a table mat depicting Ye Olde Fighting Cocks Inn at St. Albans and a cuddly hippo. If you're conducting a running feud with your neighbour, you may of course be tempted to include his prize-winning chrysanthemums on the list of items to be retrieved.

Wastepaper Basketball

Players: Any number

You will need:
A wastepaper basket, a rubber ball

This innocuous diversion keeps your guests occupied while you prepare the next big game. All you do is place a wastepaper basket next to a wall and see how many people can bounce a spongy ball once on the floor and then into the basket from a distance of around three yards. Each player is allowed three attempts, anyone who fails to score a single basket being eliminated from the competition. Those who succeed, move on to the next round where the distance increases to four yards. The distance between player and basket continues to increase with each round until there is either just one person left, or your guests are stopping traffic in order to take aim from the middle of the street.

Nose Ball

Players: 5-10

You will need:
Table tennis balls, pieces of string

If you've suffered all your life from having a big nose, this is where you finally come into your own. In this game a sizeable snout is definitely an advantage over a cute little snub nose. Lengths of string are stretched across either end of the room to denote the start and finish lines and each player places a table tennis ball on the start line. Kneeling behind their ball, they then have to nuzzle it along the course, the winner being the first to cross the finish line. If competitors are caught using any part of their anatomy other than their nose they will have to return to the start. Sneezing is also forbidden.

Obstacle Course

Players: Any number

You will need:
Blindfolds

A great favourite with practical jokers, this game can only be played once with the same group of people because it's an experience they're unlikely ever to forget. An obstacle course is laid out in the lounge, complete with tipped-up chairs, glassware, the best china tea service, marbles and drawing pins. Volunteers are enlisted and are led around the course once before being taken away to another room and blindfolded. In their absence, all of the obstacles are cleared away. Blissfully unaware of the subterfuge, the first blindfolded volunteer is brought in and taken gingerly around the non-existent course by one of the devious party goers. After stepping delicately over thin air and ducking under imaginary dangers, the poor victim is finally told that the ordeal is over. Only when the blindfold is removed does acute embarrassment sink in. When composure has been regained, the victim derives enormous pleasure from leading in the next unsuspecting performer. The game continues until the novelty wears off.

What's the Time, Mr. Wolf?

Players: 6 or more

This extremely silly game can be played either indoors or out. One player is chosen to be Mr. Wolf and stands at one end of the room or lawn whilst the others, who are all rabbits, stand at the other end behind a marker line. The confrontation begins with the rabbits all calling out: 'What's the time, Mr. Wolf?' (Now you know why you need a few drinks to play this game). Mr. Wolf replies: 'Two o'clock' or 'six o'clock' or any number up to 12. Whichever number the wolf calls out, the rabbits take the corresponding number of bunny hops forward. After a few goes, the rabbits will be quite close to Mr.

Wolf and it is then that his reply to the standard question might suddenly change to 'dinner time'. Hearing those dreaded words, the rabbits turn tail and scurry back towards the safety of their line. Any caught by Mr. Wolf before reaching sanctuary are enlisted as trainee wolves and thereafter may also devour rabbits on the call of 'dinner time'. The winner is the last rabbit left alive.

The Bell Game

Players: Any number

You will need:
Blindfolds, rolled-up newspapers, bells

Another faintly ridiculous game, this sees sensible adults, pillars of the community perhaps, trying to swat someone with rolled-up newspapers while wearing blindfolds. To add to the sense of folly, their victim has bells on. The game begins with all players but one being blindfolded and given a rolled-up newspaper. The player who is not blindfolded has a string of small bells hanging around his or her neck. As the action gets under way, the blindfolded players listen carefully to ascertain the precise whereabouts of the bells and endeavour to bash the jingling one with their newspapers while the latter attempts to dodge their blows. In the event of a direct hit, the successful assailant takes over the bells and the victim joins the blindfolded attackers. Note: any morris dancers present may take offence at this game.

Conundrums

Players: Any number

You will need:
Pieces of card, pencils and paper

Write out a selection of a dozen or more riddles, such as: 'When is a door not a door? — when it's ajar' or 'Why don't elephants like penguins? — because they can't get the wrappers off'. Give each question a number and each answer a letter and then scatter them on separate pieces of card around the house. Next, give the players 20 minutes to pair off the correct combinations by writing down the relevant number and letter. There are no short cuts, for even if they know the answer to the riddle, they still have to find the letter of the card on which it is written.

Citrus Challenge

Players: 5-10

You will need:
Lemons, tablespoons, two lengths of string

The two pieces of string are placed at opposite ends of the room, one acting as the start line, the other as a turning line. Each player is given a lemon and a tablespoon and, touching the lemon only with their spoon, must roll the fruit from the start to the turning line and back again, the first to do so being the winner. As an alternative to an individual race, this noble sport can be staged as a team relay.

Crummock

Players: 10 or more

You will need:
A supply of hats, umbrellas and children's spades, tennis ball or cabbage

The list of requirements suggests immediately that 'Crummock' is no ordinary game. Played in a garden or large room, it is a cross between hockey, lacrosse, hurling and *The Clothes Show*. The basic premise is conventional enough. There are two teams, a goal at either end of the pitch and the object is to put the ball into the opposing goal. However, the implement for hitting the ball is decidedly unorthodox and is basically anything that comes to hand. Devices have included umbrellas, children's spades and cricket stumps. Garden spades should be avoided for safety reasons. And whilst the game is usually played with a ball, the more avant-garde may prefer to use a cabbage or firm rounded lettuce. There is one more rule — players must wear a hat at all times. If you lose your headgear at any stage of the match, you are not allowed to continue until you have somehow managed to acquire a replacement. Consequently some players spend the whole game knocking off opponent's hats rather than pursuing the ball. It can surely only be a matter of time before Sky acquire the TV rights to 'Crummock'.

Blind Man's Buff

Players: Any number

You will need:
A blindfold

Arguably the oldest party game of all, 'Blind Man's Buff' remains a firm favourite with players of all ages. One player is blindfolded and staggers around the room trying to lay hands on any of the other participants. If someone is caught, the blindfolded person has to guess who it is. A correct guess results in the two exchanging places.

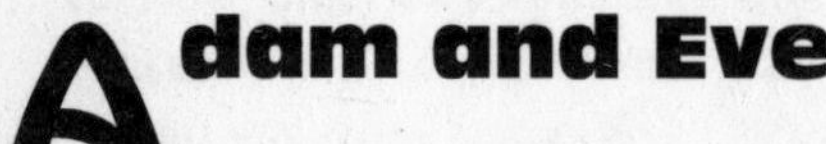

Adam and Eve

Players: Any number

You will need:
A blindfold

Of all the variations of Blind Man's Buff, this is one of the most entertaining. All but two of the players stand in a large circle holding hands. Inside the circle are a boy and a girl representing Adam and Eve, although fig leaves are optional. The boy, alias Adam, is blindfolded. The game starts with him calling out: 'Eve!' — to which she must reply: 'Over here, Adam!' He then gropes around in the dark trying to catch her. Whenever he calls for her, she must answer and she must remain within the circle. There is a time limit of two minutes and if Adam fails to catch Eve within that period, he keeps his blindfold and she changes places with another girl. If, on the other hand, Adam apprehends Eve in time, he hands his blindfold to her and swaps places with another boy. Eve then has to try to catch the new Adam. With the right people, this game has been known to lead to deep and meaningful relationships.

Footloose

Players: Any number

After removing their shoes and putting them in the middle of the room, players plunge into the pile in an unseemly *mêlée* and mix up the footwear. Then everyone retreats to the corners of the room to wait for the lights to be switched off. Once the room is in total darkness, the scrum begins again as the players have just two minutes in which to find their shoes and put them on the correct feet. This game can get a little rough and is therefore not ideal for spinsters of the parish and maiden aunts, unless they happen to be black belts in karate.

My Mother's Cake

Players: Any even number

Two teams sit in rows facing each other with their legs outstretched so that their feet are touching (this game can be played barefoot if desired). Each player is given the name of an ingredient in a cake recipe. The host then tells a story about how the cake was made, in the course of which the various ingredients are referred to. Whenever players hear the name of their ingredient, they must run up between the two lines, vaulting over the outstretched legs, before running back down behind their team to return to their original place. The fun starts when there are two or three ingredients mentioned in quick succession, all racing around at the same time, and when a player sits down breathlessly, only to be forced into action again straight away.

Hop, Step, Jump and Crawl

Players: 6 or more

This game is an admirable test of players' ingenuity... as well as making them look remarkably silly. The participants line up elbow to elbow and the first in the line moves forward a few yards in a distinctive manner — maybe a John Cleese silly walk, or by hopping, crawling, walking backwards, bottom shuffling or, for the particularly athletic, walking on their hands. Each of the other players in turn must then move forward the same distance but by a different method to any previous competitor. And so the game continues in rotation with every player trying to think of some new form of motion. Anyone who fails to come up with something new is eliminated. The last player left in is the winner.

Birds of a Feather

Players: 5-10

You will need:
Feathers, plates

Each player is given a plate with a feather on it and on the command 'Go!' they have to race to the finish line while taking care not to lose their feather. The plate must be held at the side so that the hands have no contact with the feather. The use of glue to stick the feather to the plate is also forbidden. The game is definitely a case of more haste less speed because if the feather drifts away during the race, that player has to return to the start. The winner is the first person to cross the finish line with the feather still on the plate.

Incongruities

Players: Any number

You will need:
Pencils and paper

This game tests your guests' powers of observation. Prepare for the game by placing familiar objects in strange places around the house — such as a razor on the mantelpiece or a mustard dish in the bathroom. All objects must be in full view. Give each player pencil and paper and send them around the house in search of as many incongruities as they can find in 10 minutes. The one to spot the most things out of place is the winner. This game does not work well in a naturally untidy house...

Grand National

Players: 6 or more

You will need:
Potatoes, brooms, paper plates, chairs, a length of string

This is a silly relay game in which teams have to ride a broomstick to a turning line and back while balancing a potato on a plate on their head. Players are allowed to grip the plate with one hand but must not hold down the potato. If the potato falls off, they have to pick it up before they can continue. To make things even more interesting for spectators, tie a length of string between two chairs, about a foot off the ground, to form a fence half-way round the course. This obstacle has to be jumped by the competitors. As they complete the course, the racers hand their broomstick, potato and plate over to the next member of their team. The game continues in this fashion until all the members of one team have fully negotiated the course successfully. With three or more 'horses' racing round at the same time, there are frequent fallers, refusals and even stewards' inquiries.

Socks Appeal

Players: 5-10

You will need:
Pairs of socks, pairs of thick gloves, blindfolds

Before you play this game, you will need to provide an assortment of old socks and thick gloves, one pair of gloves per player. These should be unwieldy garments such as gardening gloves or oven gloves. The socks are piled up in the middle of the room and players are told to put a glove on each hand, but not a matching pair. The players are then blindfolded. On the command 'Go!', they must locate the pile of socks and, still gloved, put on as many pairs of socks as they can in a time limit of 10 minutes. The player wearing the most socks at the end of the10 minutes, wins the game. If any blindfolded competitor has difficulty finding the pile in the first place, he or she can be discreetly pointed in the right direction.

Crocodile Race

Players: 10 or more

Players divide into teams of equal numbers and form lines at one end of the room. They then squat on their heels and place their hands on the shoulders or waist of the person in front to form a stunningly realistic crocodile. When the signal is given to start the race, the crocodiles move forward in jumps and bounces until they reach the far end of the room. There they must turn and head back to the start/finish line. If at any time in the race a player loses contact with the person in front, that team must stop and regroup. To do this, the tail end of the crocodile must stay where it is while the front end goes back to join it. The reputation of the crocodile as a mean, efficient speed machine can be severely damaged by this game.

Guess the Leader

Players: Any number

Depending on the personnel involved, 'Guess the Leader' can either be a gentle, sedate game or decidedly raucous and unruly. It begins with one player being sent out of the room — he or she becomes the guesser. Meanwhile, the others gather round and choose a leader who explains that, from then on, they must follow precisely whatever the leader does. When the guesser returns, he or she has to observe the various actions performed by the group and decide which of them is the leader. At first the leader's movements will probably be relatively simple — a spot of hand clapping and arm waving — but they may become increasingly curious, incorporating rolling around on the floor with legs in the air, impersonating Long John Silver or rubbing bottoms with the person next in line. Unless you all happen to be particularly close friends, anything stronger than nibbling ear lobes is inadvisable. The key to success is for the leader to switch actions when the guesser is studying the other players. When the leader is identified, he or she assumes the role of guessing.

Balloon Fight

Players: Any number

You will need:
Balloons, newspapers, pieces of string

Even at the height of Culloden, Waterloo or Bosworth Field, the ferocity of combat did not match that of the average balloon fight. Each player ties a balloon to his or her ankle with a piece of string and, wielding a rolled-up newspaper, endeavours to defend the balloon against other players' attempts to burst it while simultaneously trying to burst theirs. No balloons may be burst by hand or by sharp implements. Any player who does suffer the ignominy of a burst balloon is eliminated, the last player left is declared the winner.

TV Titles

Players: 4-15

You will need:
Pieces of card, pencils and paper

Compile a list of about 40 well-known television programmes (all with more than one-word titles) and split the titles in half as in *LAST OF THE/SUMMER WINE*. Write all of the second halves on separate pieces of card and distribute them in cunningly concealed places around the house. Give each player the first half of a title and send him or her away to find the slip bearing the second half. When the appropriate second section has been located, the player brings it back to you and is issued with a new title to find. The winner is the player who has tracked down most titles when you call time (a period of 20 minutes is reasonable).

Marble Race

Players: 4-8

You will need:
Pencils, marbles, blindfolds

Blindfolded players have to carry a marble balanced on two pencils along an indoor course with at least one bend in it. The pencils must be held with arms outstretched. Onlookers may assist in verbally steering the players in the right direction and can also replace any dropped marbles on to the pencils. This event works best as a knock-out competition with two players racing against each other, the winner progressing to the next round.

Bang

Players: Any even number

You will need:
Chairs, a cushion

The principal requirement to playing this game successfully is an ability not to betray your emotions through the expression on your face. Players are split into two teams who sit opposite each other. To one side of the room is a chair with a cushion on it. Each team writes the names of the opposing team members on separate slips of paper. Team A then places one of the slips beneath the cushion and invites any member of team B to go and sit on that chair. The aim of the game is to avoid sitting on your own name. If you do, the opposing team chorus loudly: 'Bang!' and you are effectively dead and therefore out of the game. If it is not your name however, you return to your team unscathed. It is then team B's turn to select a name to be put under the cushion and so the game continues until one team has been completely wiped out. The important thing is not to appear too excited when you know that any of your opponents are about to sit on their own name. For seasoned performers will be on the lookout for telltale signs even as they lower their bottom into position. If they suspect something is amiss, they can pull out at the last minute and return to their team, as long as buttocks and cushion have not actually come into contact.

Peanut Hunt

Players: Any number

You will need:
Peanuts, paper bags, blindfolds

Pigs at feeding time pale in comparison to the undignified sight of adults scrambling about the floor hunting for peanuts. The players are blindfolded, given a paper bag and told to search for the peanuts which are scattered around the room. After five minutes of frantic activity, the blindfolds are removed and a count is made to see who has collected the most peanuts. The game works best with large numbers of people, particularly when five or six converge on the same stray peanut.

Back-to-Back Race

Players: Any even number

Players form pairs and line up at one end of the room back-to-back with their arms linked. At the off, they must race to the far end of the room and back again, keeping their arms linked at all times. Any couple who become untangled must return to the start. Where possible, it is always advisable for the front runner to be the heavier partner in each pair as he or she will have to do any pulling. A slim girl dragging along a burly hod carrier could result in a fairly slow lap time.

Hobby Horse

Players: Any even numbers

Few people of sound mind would attempt this game but, if sufficient alcohol has been consumed beforehand, that is unlikely to disqualify any of your company from taking part. It sounds simple enough — players have to carry their fellow team members across the room one by one — but the catch is that the same method of transportation cannot be employed twice by the same team. So whilst the first carriers will probably play reasonably safe with fireman's lifts and piggy backs, the last to go have to come up with something infinitely more imaginative. Styles such as piggy back front-to-front suggest that mating is imminent and could lead to disquiet in some quarters, as could the sight of collapsed couples writhing around on the floor. Those with hernias should opt to be baggage.

The Wardrobe Game

Players: Any number

You will need:

Two overnight bags, four night-caps, four large nightdresses, four pairs of slippers, four dressing-gowns

Players are split up into two teams which are then sub-divided into pairs. The first couple in each team are given an overnight bag containing two night-caps, two large nightdresses, two pairs of slippers and two dressing-gowns. Starting from one end of the room, they have to carry their bags to two chairs situated at the opposite end, take off their shoes, put on the night-caps, nightdresses, slippers and dressing-gowns, run round their chair once, take all the nightclothes off again, put their own shoes back on, repack their bags and race back to the start where they hand over to the next couple. The relay continues until the final couple in one team cross the finish line complete with repacked bag. The sight of grown men running around in nightdresses is more than enough justification for including this game in your party. The worrying time is when they appear to be enjoying it.

Pass the Bonnet

Players: Any even number

You will need:

Two large bonnets, two large pairs of bedsocks

This is another dressing-up game which can cause a certain amount of embarrassment to the more staid members of the male community. To ensure the maximum unease, you need to prepare two outrageous bonnets with ribbons, the sort of headgear that Mrs. Shilling used to wear at Royal Ascot. Instead of the traditional fruit, why not go for a bonnet laden with vegetables? How about parsnips, beetroot and carrots with the odd cucumber thrown in for good effect, and topped by a huge model wheelbarrow? Whatever you come up with, divide the players into two teams and line them up in rows for an exciting contest. The first player in each team dons the bonnet, tying it beneath the chin and, after removing shoes, puts on an outsize pair of bedsocks. The second player then undoes the ribbons, puts on the bonnet, ties the ribbons, removes his or her shoes and player one's bedsocks and puts on the bedsocks. It carries on like this along the line until every team member has worn the bonnet and bedsocks, at which point that team is declared the winner.

Rabbit Race

Players: 2-6

You will need:
Cardboard, chairs, lengths of string

There is nothing like a fast, all-action race to bring the party to fever pitch, even if the participants are nothing more than cardboard rabbits. The first thing you need to do to prepare for this game is to cut out the rabbits. There must be one rabbit per player and they should be identical in every respect — no sticking a fluffy cotton wool bobtail onto one because it will slow it down. Lastly pierce a hole in the centre of each bunny's head — it may sound cruel, but remember they are only cardboard. Once you have made your racing rabbits, line up a row of chairs — one for for each rabbit — and tie a length of string, about twelve feet long, to the back of each chair. Thread the strings through the holes in the rabbits' heads and place the animals at the start line. Now the players take over. At the off, they seize the loose end of the string and, by relaxing and tightening the string, the rabbit is inched forward towards the chair. For swifter progress, it is important that the rabbit should be inclined slightly towards the chair. Having reached the chair, the rabbits must turn for home. To make the rabbits change direction, the players need to waggle the string and tighten and relax it quickly. Again ensure that the rabbit is leaning towards the direction in which it is supposed to be heading. The first player to get his or her rabbit back to the start line wins a *Fatal Attraction* video.

Identical Twins

Players: Any number

You will need:
Two packs of playing cards

This is a team game in which players have to search the house for hidden playing cards. Before the party, you should place all 52 cards from one pack in various places around the house. However, they should not be concealed to the extent that guests have to set about demolishing your home in order to reach the ace of spades. Instead have one card protruding slightly from the pages of a book or another resting beneath an ornament — but not a valuable family heirloom. The game starts with each player being given a playing card and told to find its identical twin. When a card is found and returned to you, make a note of that person's team and give him or her another card to locate. At the end of the time limit (around 20 minutes is ideal) tot up the points to find out which team is the winner. Players will soon learn to make a mental note of any other card they stumble across while searching for their own, just in case they have to look for that one later. And, of course, they can help their team mates by telling them where a certain card is hidden. It might be best to whisper such information lest the enemy be listening in.

Waiter!

Players: Any number

You will need:
Table tennis balls, paper plates

In this team game, the members stand in lines with just enough space between each player to allow one of their number to weave in and out at speed. The first player carries a paper plate in the reverse palm of his or her hand — waiter-fashion. On the plate is a table tennis ball, denoting the

breakfast egg. That player must run in and out of his or her team mates, announcing to each: 'Your breakfast is served, sir (or madam).' When he or she completes the slalom course and runs back to the starting point, the plate and table tennis ball are handed over to the second player who sets off on a new run with player one becoming the first person in the new line. If the ball is dropped at any stage (and no hands can be used to hold it down), the player has to go back to the start of that run. The first team to have every player complete the run wins the game.

Nuts and Apples

Players: Any number

You will need:
Nuts, apples, teaspoons, knives

Give each player a teaspoon and a blunt knife and ask them to stand at the opposite end of the room to a large table laden with assorted nuts and small apples. On the command 'Go!', they run over to the table with the spoon in their left hand and the knife in their right and attempt to scoop a nut onto the knife and an apple into the teaspoon. Obviously, with a mighty Granny Smith this is nigh on impossible, so smaller varieties should be provided. With both foodstuffs in place, the players must then dash back to the start/finish line, the first to cross it with nut and apple intact being the winner. Anyone who drops either item must get down on their hands and knees and try to recover it. This has been known to take some time. In fact, if you come downstairs the following morning and find any hapless guest still on all fours struggling to retrieve their nut and apple, it is kindest to put them out of their misery and allow them to go home.

Peg-in-the-Bottle

Players: Any number

You will need:
Clothes pegs, empty milk bottles

A game of undoubted skill, this is eminently suitable for the less athletic among your guests. Divide the players into teams of four and supply each team with an empty milk bottle (a jamjar will do) and 12 clothes pegs. Taking it in turns, each player stands with their feet together a couple of inches behind their team's bottle and tries to drop the clothes pegs into the bottle from the height of their nose. They must keep their feet together and hold their body up straight. Each player is allowed three attempts and any peg which misses may not be used again. When each of the players has had their go, the victorious team is calculated by adding up the total number of pegs in each bottle.

Whistle For Your Supper

Players: Any number

You will need:
A supply of water biscuits, chairs

Players line up in equal-numbered teams on the opposite side of the room to a row of chairs (one per team). The game starts with the first players in each team running over to the appropriate chair, sitting down on it and eating a water biscuit as quickly as possible. Having devoured the *whole* biscuit, they must then try to whistle. The sound doesn't have to be as clear as a Roger Whittaker solo, but it must be a definite whistle rather than just a blow. When the judge approves the whistling note, they race back to their line and hand over to the next player. And so it continues until one team has finished.

Witch Hunt

Players: Any number

In truth this is nothing more than an excuse for adults to play hide and seek but what's wrong with that? One player is chosen to be the witch and, after turning off all of the lights, goes away to find a suitable place to hide. Five minutes later, the witch hunters set off in pursuit, still in total darkness. As they stumble around the furniture, they are allowed two cries of 'Where are you, Witchy?' to which the witch must reply with an eerie cackle. But there is nothing to prevent the witch moving somewhere else after each cackle. Whoever eventually succeeds in catching the witch dons the mantle for the next instalment. To add to the atmosphere, it is a nice touch to supply the witch with a pointed hat and a cloak. However, the authenticity should stop there and under no circumstances should any attempt be made to carry out Trial by Ordeal.

General Post

Players: Any number

You will need:
A blindfold, chairs

All of the players except one sit in a circle and call out the name of a town which is written down by you, the postmaster. The other person is placed in the middle of the circle and blindfolded. The postmaster then chooses two towns and announces: 'The post is going from Chipping Sodbury to Arbroath' or wherever. At that point, the two players whose towns are Chipping Sodbury and Arbroath must rush to change places without being caught by the person in the blindfold. Anyone who is caught takes a turn in the middle. But the greatest pandemonium occurs when the postmaster suddenly calls out: 'General Post!', for then every player must find a new seat without being caught and the country's post ends up in a bigger mess than it is anyway.

Pancake Race

Players: 6-12

You will need:
Squares of newspaper, garden canes

For this ingenious re-enactment of Shrove Tuesday, you will need two pieces of newspaper, about a foot square, and four garden canes, each around three feet long. Each square of paper represents a pancake and two canes, held one in each hand, represent a frying pan. The players are divided into two teams and their aim is to pick up a 'pancake' from the floor at one end of the room with the 'frying pan' and carry it as quickly as they can to a table at the other end of the room. They then have to pick up the 'pancake' again, transfer it back to its original place on the floor and hand over to the next team member... and so on until one team has finished. Patience is definitely a virtue in this game as any hurried movement will result in your 'pancake' floating out of the 'pan'. So steady progress is the order of the day.

Wobbly Bosoms

Players: Any number

You will need:
Balloons filled with water

Unless you are prepared for a soaking, 'Wobbly Bosoms' calls for steady nerves and even steadier hands. Some homeowners would prefer to play this game outside, or at least on an easily mopped surface. Fill a number of balloons with water and carefully seal them up. Then gather all the players close together and start a nice gentle game of catch. Anyone who flinches at the crucial moment of catching the water-filled balloon risks either dropping it or, worse still, having it explode on them. In either case the penalty is elimination from the game. The winner of the game is the driest at the end.

Stepping Stones

Players: 8 or more

You will need:
Shoeboxes

This is a team game where half of each team stand at one end of the room with the other half at the opposite end. The first player in each team is given two lidless shoeboxes and the race gets under way with him or her tossing one of the boxes on the floor a short distance in front. Stepping into the box with the left foot, he or she then raises the right foot off the ground and, balancing on the left, places the second box on the floor a little further forward. He or she then steps into that second box with the right foot and then balances on the right while turning to pick up the first box and lobbing that a little further up the course. And so it continues until he or she reaches the far end and hands over to the second member of the team. The game is over when all the members of one team have stepped gingerly from end to end. If any player loses balance and touches the floor with either hand or with the foot that is supposed to be off the floor, he or she must pick up both boxes and go back to start that leg of the race all over again. If you haven't got any shoeboxes, or if you're a secret hula-hoop champion, this game can be played equally well with cardboard squares or plastic hoops.

Pairs

Players: 5-10

You will need:
Various matching items

Before the party, hide one item of a pair somewhere around the house. The pairs can either be identical ornaments or associated articles such as knife and fork, pepper and salt pots, pen and pencil. At the start, give each player one half of a pair and instruct him or her to find the other half. If, in the course of their travels, players stumble across someone else's quarry, they are advised to keep quiet. Nobody cares about the winner in this game (after all, it could be over in a matter of seconds) but the loser is the last person to find his or her pair and is consequently subjected to a forfeit.

Orange-Hopping

Players: 5-10

You will need:
Spoons, oranges, two lengths of string, chairs

Construct a circular racecourse featuring two fences made from a length of string tied about 18 inches off the ground between two chairs. The runners line up at the start on one leg with each one carrying a spoon in their left hand. On the floor, in front of them, are a line of oranges. At a signal, they pick up their orange with the spoon without touching the ground with their hands or their non-standing foot. They then set off hopping around the course, orange and spoon in hand. If any oranges are dropped, they must be picked up with the spoon. The winner is the first to complete two circuits.

Four-Legged Race

Players: Teams of 3

You will need:
Lengths of rope or strong twine

A step up from the traditional three-legged race, the 'four-legged race' features teams of three. This means that the right leg of the centre member of the team is strapped to the left leg of the team-mate on the right and the centre player's left leg is tied to the right leg of the team-mate on the left. The teams limp along the course (which should either be the length of a room or in the garden) and the first to cross the finishing line with their legs still strapped are the winners, regardless of whether they are standing, crawling on all fours or writhing along on their stomachs like demented snakes.

True or False

Players: Any even number

You will need:
Plenty of chairs

Two teams sit on chairs facing each other. At either end of the room, between the two rows, is an empty chair. One is the 'true' chair, the other the 'false' chair. The host makes a statement to each pair of players in turn. If they think the statement is true, they run to the 'true' chair, if they think it's not, they run to the 'false' chair. Whoever sits on the correct seat wins a point for their team. When both players dash to the same chair, the first to be seated wins the point. The best statements to use are ones which are open to confusion, such as 'Harry H. Corbett operated Sooty.' (Harry Corbett operated Sooty, Harry H. Corbett starred in *Steptoe and Son*).

Balloon Relay

Players: Any even number

You will need:
Wire clothes-hangers, balloons, garden canes, chairs

Arrange two pairs of chairs in opposite corners of the room, one pair for each team. Over the back of each chair hook a coat-hanger and wedge a balloon onto the horizontal rung of the hanger. Using only a piece of garden cane (preferably without half the garden still attached to it), the players have to release the balloon from its resting place, guide it over to the opposite chair and force it onto the shelf of the coat hanger there. Then the next player takes over and so on until every member of one team has successfully transported the balloon from one chair to the other. For once, there is no penalty if the balloon hits the floor.

Cat and Mouse

Players: 2

You will need:
Blindfolds

Even though it is only for two players, this is the perfect way to round off a dinner party as the spectators will have as much fun as the participants. It is played round the table with a male guest chosen to be the cat and a girl to be the mouse. If any guests think that is sexist or rodentist, feel free to reverse the roles. Both players are blindfolded, spun around three times and steered towards the table, but neither is told where the other is. The game itself should be played in total silence with the cat listening intently for any hint of mouse and vice-versa. When the cat does finally catch his prey, another pair of *Tom and Jerrys* will be only too keen to take over.

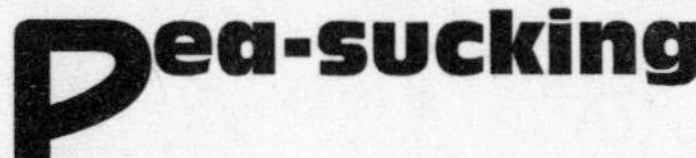

Pea-sucking

Players: 4 or more

You will need:
Dried peas, straws, saucers

Three saucers are set out in the room, one at either end and one in the middle. One of the end ones contains a number of dried peas. On the command 'Go!', the first member of each team lifts a pea from the full saucer by sucking it through a straw. With the pea held like that, the team member runs over to the saucer in the middle of the room and drops the pea there. At the middle saucer a team-mate takes over and, in the same fashion, completes the transfer to the far end of the room. The team that switches most peas from one end of the room to the other in five minutes wins the game. Anyone caught blowing through the straw instead of sucking is liable to a stern reprimand and a bill for any damage.

Hunt the Thimble

Players: Any number

You will need:
A thimble

A classic party game in which all of the players except one leave the room while the remaining one hides a thimble. Whilst the thimble shouldn't stick out like a sore thumb, it be too heavily concealed, either. The other players return to search for the thimble. When they locate it, they don't say anything but just sit down quietly. The last player to find the thimble is the loser and has to hide it for the next round. There are no winners in this game. If your household is a thimble-free zone, you can use any small object in its place... as long as you remember to tell your guests what they are looking for.

Up for the Cup

Players: 3-8

You will need:
Paper cups, paper plates

If you can excel at this game, it's a sure sign that you haven't had nearly enough to drink, for it is a contest which requires the lightest touch and perfect balance. Set out a small table at either end of the room. On one table stack a pile of paper plates; on the other a pile of paper cups. The object of the game is simple, but the execution is more difficult. Beginning with a plate, then a cup, then another plate, the players have to build the highest possible tower of alternate plates and cups, walking between the two tables to acquire fresh items. While on the move, their hands must only hold the bottom plate. If at any point their tower collapses, they have to go back to the plate table and start all over again. The player with the tallest tower at the end of five minutes wins the game.

Word Search

Players: Any number

You will need:
Slips of paper

Before the party, think up a list of words of six letters, one word per player. Write the individual letters on separate slips of paper and scatter them around the house. Each word should have its own identifying number and this should be written on the pieces of paper. Thus if 'CASUAL' is word number one, the slips of paper bearing C,A,S,U,A and L should all carry the number one. Each player is handed a piece of paper giving details of the mystery word which he or she has to find. The information on the paper will also reveal the number of letters in the word and that word's identifying number. The players then go off to find their letters and work out their word. The first to do so wins the game.

Medley Relay

Players: Any even number

You will need:
Bananas, balloons, potatoes, chairs

In this crazy relay, couples compete against each other in a series of strange tasks. The race starts with the men and women lined up on opposite sides of the room. A row of chairs (one per couple) are arranged on the men's side. First, each man has to devour a banana, run to his female partner, kneel before her and hum a pre-designated tune. When the girl guesses the tune, she blows up a balloon, knots it, runs over to the chair and bursts the balloon by sitting on it. She then runs back to join her partner and, with a potato wedged between their foreheads, they shuffle across the floor together back to the chair. If the potato falls, they have to start that activity again. The race is over when the girl is seated in the chair with her man standing beside her.

Butter Fingers

Players: 3-6

You will need:
Oven gloves (one pair per player), milk bottle tops, cardboard boxes with lids

Any man who has ever fumbled with a recalcitrant bra strap will know only too well the sensation of helplessness which can be experienced during this game. The competitors line up at one end of the room, all wearing oven gloves, ideally the sort which are joined together. They run to the other end and try to pick up a milk bottle top, which they then carry back to the start line where a row of cardboard boxes fitted with ballot-box style slots have been arranged. After posting the bottle top (no easy feat in oven gloves!), they go back for another one. The winner is the player with most successfully-posted bottle tops in three minutes. As a prize, he or she gets to keep the oven gloves.

Strip Tease

Players: Any number

You will need:
Streamers, sticky-backed paper

There's no need to worry about any of your guests' blood pressure — this game is by no means as risqué as it sounds, as becomes clear when you realise that the strips in question are strips of streamer. Prior to the party, cut the streamers into various lengths, from about two to eight inches, and hide them around the house in such a way that only the ends are visible. Next, cut some sticky-backed paper into small squares and put them in a dish. All the players have to do is scour the house for pieces of streamer and then stick them together with the adhesive paper. Whoever manages to assemble the longest streamer in 10 minutes is the winner.

That Shallot

Players: Teams of 4

You will need:
Pickled onions, teaspoons

This hardly bears thinking about. Players are divided into equal teams, each member of which is given a teaspoon. The first player in each team holds a bowl replete with pickled onions and, on the signal to start, feeds two onions to the next player in line. When both onions have been eaten, and there is positively no sign of munching, player two takes the bowl and feeds player three with a pair of pickles. And so it continues, slowly and painfully, until player one has devoured the two offerings from player four. When deciding whether to include this game, it is important to take two matters into consideration — firstly, that none of the players have an inbuilt aversion to pickled onions and secondly, that there are no more close contact games planned for the rest of the evening.

The Great Feather Race

Players: Teams of 4

You will need:
4 feathers, 4 small tables

Clear away the valuable furniture and choose four teams, each comprising of anything up to half a dozen members. They position themselves in the four corners of the room. Each team is issued with a small feather, the aim being to be the first to blow the feather across the room and land it on a table which is situated in the opposite corner. The four teams each start at the same time, so there is the prospect of 24 people converging on the centre of the room, all frantically trying to keep their team's feathers airborne. If a feather falls to the floor, it must be picked up and re-started from the same spot. If any player is seen transporting the feather illegally — by hand, head, shoulder, mouth or any other part of the anatomy — that team will automatically be disqualified. Anyone player who inadvertently swallows a feather will be treated more leniently, probably in hospital.

FOR BUDDING OLIVIERS

Charades

Players: Any number

Championed on TV by the long-running *Give Us A Clue*, Charades has enjoyed a resurgence of popularity in recent years. And deservedly so. – because with the right group of people, there are few more entertaining party games. The aim of the most common form of 'Charades' is to mime the title of a film, play, TV programme, song or book, but the rules can also be applied to ordinary words or phrases. Although the performance must be silent, a number of visual aids can be employed.

Film – The right hand cranks an imaginary movie camera

Play – Sweep each hand downward in an arc to represent stage curtains

TV programme– Draw a square in the air with both forefingers

Song – Put both hands to your mouth and release imaginary words. Born crooners may additionally choose to go down on one knee with a glazed look on their face, clasping their heart. This does not indicate an impending coronary but a tender ballad.

Book – Two hands are placed together and opened palm up.

Number of words – Hold up the appropriate number of fingers.

The first word of the mime – If you are starting with the third word, hold up three fingers and so on

Number of syllables – Tap the relevant number of fingers on your forearm

The whole thing – If you are describing everything in one go, draw a large circle in the air with your arms.

Sounds like – Tug gently at your earlobe

A short word – For words such as 'a', 'an', 'the', 'on', 'but', 'in' and 'of', hold an invisible space between your thumb and forefinger and wait until someone guesses the correct word.

A correct guess – point vigorously at that person

When a mime is guessed correctly, the successful player performs the next mime, unless you're playing 'Team Charades', in which case your team scores a point and the next group has a go. If you're preparing a list of titles in advance, it's fun to tailor them to your guests' personalities. So the vicar gets to mime *White Punks On Dope*, or *Fanny by Gaslight*.

nimal Charades

Players: Any number

In this version of 'Charades', players act out the names of animal or birds. This should be done by a combination of word miming and silent actions. Extroverts will relish the opportunity to bound around like a kangaroo; while quieter guests may prefer the three-toed sloth... although this can lead to an extremely long game. For a trick version of this, place slips of paper into a hat which all bear the same animal's name. Amid the utmost secrecy, each player picks out a slip, then one person is sent from the room to prepare the mime. When he or she returns, the other players – all of whom know what the animal is – deliberately avoid guessing the mime. It can be mildly amusing to watch a poor guest desperately trying to convey 'donkey', even to the point of eating a carrot, while all around are guessing goat, horse, cow, hippopotamus etc.

Proverbial Panto

Players: Any number

You will need:
Pencils and paper

Players are divided into two teams, each person writing down a proverb on a piece of paper. The teams then exchange the slips and players take it in turns to act out the proverbs they have been given. If their team mates guess the proverb correctly, that team gains a point. If the proverb isn't solved, it's passed across for the other team to guess.

Shadow Play

Players: Any number

You will need:
A large white sheet, a lamp, two chairs

Two volunteers stand on chairs, holding the ends of a large white sheet. Positioned behind the sheet should be a bright light so that whoever is between the wall and sheet casts a clear, sharp shadow onto the sheet. The players act in pairs and, using the sheet as a screen, perform a short silent routine for everyone else to guess. This could take the form of a nursery rhyme, a proverb or a song title. Given the limitations of the medium, attempting to perform the whole of Act Two from *King Lear* by shadow acting is probably a trifle ambitious.

Superheroes

Players: 4-8

Players take it in turns to assume the identity of various superheroes, either of their own creation or that of the host, and invite the other players to guess their name. The actors may speak but must not use the words contained in their name. Thus Television Repair Man may use every word in the English language with the exception of 'television' and 'repair'. Imagination is the key to the game. Avoid the likes of Batman, Spiderman and Superman and opt for less obvious heroes such as Coffee Percolator Man, Gravy Granule Man and Gerbil Woman.

libi

Players: 5 or more

If you are a devotee of murder whodunnits and reckon you can crack the strongest alibi, this game will go down a storm at your party. Two players (the accused) are sent from the room and given 10 minutes to concoct an alibi for an imaginary crime. Their story should cover a specific time – say two hours – and they can refuse to answer any questions which do not relate to that period. Once they have agreed upon their version of events, one of the pairs returns to the room to be subjected to five minutes' interrogation from the rest of the guests (the prosecution). The second defendant is then sent for and, over the next five minutes, is questioned intensely as the prosecution attempt to throw up discrepancies in the two defendants' alibis. If at any point the second defendant fails to corroborate the first's story, they lose the game and have to do a forfeit.

Proposals

Players: 6-12

You will need:
Pencils and paper

Should you feel that your party is getting too cosy, a quick game of 'Proposals' might help to stir things up a bit. Ideally there should be an equal number of men and women playing this game although watching two heterosexual men declaring their undying love for one another can be amusing. Then again it is probably no more than they do after seven pints on a lads' night out. Everyone writes their name on a piece of paper and puts the slip in a pile (one for men, the other for women). The names are then paired off and one of each pair has to get down on bended knee and propose marriage to the other. This can be invigorating if you find yourself proposing to someone you've always lusted after... and downright dangerous if your partner is watching your every move.

Dumb Crambo

Players: Any even number

An old favourite in which two teams sit facing one another. One team selects a word to be mimed by the other but before they can mime it they must find out what the word is. This has to be done by trial and error, the only help they receive being when the captain of the first team gives them a word which rhymes with the mystery word. Then the members of the guessing team take it in turns to mime what they think the word might be. So if the chosen word is 'light' and the clue given is that it rhymes with 'kite', the guessing team could mime 'night', 'might', 'write', 'height', 'bite', 'fight', 'transvestite' and so on. If any player cannot think of a word to mime, a team mate may whisper an idea, but no other words must be spoken by the guessing team, hence the name of the game. After each failed mime, the captain of the first team declares that the opponents have guessed incorrectly and the unsuccessful mime artist is roundly booed. However, a successful mime should be rewarded with a generous round of applause. Keep note of the number of mimes each team takes to guess the chosen word, each failure incurring a penalty point. At the end of the game, the team with fewest points are the winners.

Mind Readers

Players: Any even number

The players divide into two teams, one of which leaves the room. The remaining team thinks up a situation to be acted out – anything from hailing a taxi in Siberia to giving an enema – and calls in one member of the other team. Once that person has been told the situation, he or she mimes it to the next team member. This procedure continues through the team like a silent version of 'Chinese Whispers' until the action reaches the last member whose task it is to ascertain precisely what is being acted out. Obviously the more players there are, the greater the likelihood of departure from the original idea. The two teams then swap roles.

World's Worst

Players: 5-10

Before the party, think up a number of 'world's worst' categories. You then ask the players to perform suitable examples. For instance, if the subject is 'the world's worst kisser', the player may mime a horrendous tongue sandwich or simply point to her husband. Players are allowed to speak but must not use the key word, in this case 'kiss'. When everyone has exhausted a subject, move on to the next. The performer who gets the most laughs is the winner. In case you get stuck for inspiration, here are a few more subject ideas:

World's worst contagious disease
World's worst cook
World's worst football team
World's worst case of vertigo
World's worst dress sense
World's worst case of flatulence

The Railway Carriage Game

Players: 4-10

A popular exercise among wartime spy schools, 'The Railway Carriage Game' tests players' ability to detect a secret phrase. Players are divided into pairs, each member of which is given a secret phrase. They then climb into an imaginary railway carriage and talk to each other for five minutes, during which time they must slip the given phrase into the conversation as discreetly as possible. When the time is up, each must guess the other's mystery phrase. If the guess is unsuccessful, the puzzle can be thrown over to the fellow passengers. Here are a few likely phrases:

I do so enjoy the taste of Pot Noodle
My, what fascinating feet you have
I feel one of my hot flushes coming on
My pet stick insect is called Avril
Who'd have thought the Pope was once a Bay City Rollers fan

Sneaky Sentences

Players: 4-10

In this variation of 'The Railway Carriage Game', four players leave the room and think of four distinctive phrases to slip into their conversations, one per player. When the outsiders return, the other players must listen intently to their conversations and try to spot the chosen phrases.

The Plimsoll Game

Players: 5-10

A letter of the alphabet is picked and everyone writes down the name of a famous person beginning with that letter. The names are then read out in turn and, via healthy debate, the players proceed to lay claim to their chosen person being the most eminent in his or her field. Thus, if the letter selected is D, players might argue that Ken Dodd is Liverpool's finest comedian, that Kenny Dalglish is Scotland's greatest ever footballer, that Sir Francis Drake was Britain's bravest seafarer, that Benjamin Disraeli was our most accomplished Prime Minister and that Deputy Dawg was the world's finest sheriff. The game gets its name from a session where someone cited Samuel Plimsoll as the finest man ever to have lent his name to the lines on the sides of ships.

Panto

Players: 6 or more

You will need:
Assorted articles

Here is the chance to stage a pantomime in the comfort of your own home. Divide the players into teams and give each team three gloriously unconnected articles. The actors then have to perform a four-minute improvised pantomime incorporating all three articles. Try these combinations:

a sink plunger, a tea bag and a tampon
a sticking plaster, a cabbage and a golf ball
a roll-on deodorant, a mouse trap and a set of false teeth

Pandora's Box

Players: Any number

In a similar vein to Panto, 'Pandora's Box' requires individuals to weave a two-minute story around three random objects. The difference is that here they don't have to act the story, just tell it. Since the objects in question don't have to be produced, the choice is limitless but even so, some items are easier to connect than you might think. For example, a signed photograph of Paula Yates, a match and a waste-paper bin could be linked in one sentence easily. The following combinations, however, might prove more challenging:

Big Ben, a lobster and Burt Reynolds' toupee

A cardboard cut-out of Shirley Bassey, a combine harvester and a water bed

A suit of armour, a hot water bottle and an inflatable Spacehopper

Fancy Undress

Players: Any number

This is a bit of fun at fancy dress parties. For half-an-hour, guests have to behave in the manner of a famous person other than the one they are dressed as. It can be quite disconcerting talking to a man dressed as Long John Silver but acting like Wayne Sleep or to a woman who is dressed like Queen Victoria but behaves like Mae West. At the end of the half-hour, everyone must work out who is pretending to be who. The best performance wins a prize, as do the best newcomer, best supporting artist, best acceptance speech etc.

What's My Line?

Players: Any number

For the party version of this old TV favourite, prepare a list of occupations prior to playing. Make them as diverse as possible – brain surgeon, page three model, rat catcher, pizza chef. The first player is secretly given an occupation from the list and has to mime it to the others. Whoever guesses the nature of the job has the next turn. This can be also be played as a team game.

The Destination Game

Players: Any even number

One team leaves the room and chooses the name of a town or city to which its members are supposedly travelling. On their return, the individual team members take it turns to mime a letter of their destination by performing an action which begins with the appropriate letter. For example, if the destination is Rochdale, the players could try Rowing, Ordering, Cutting, Heating, Diving, Agreeing, Lifting and, for a sting in the tail, Embalming. The mimes must be performed in the correct order. When all of the mimes are completed, the other team have five minutes to try to work out the destination, during which time they can ask for a mime to be repeated. If they guess the destination, it becomes their turn to think of a town or city. If not, the first team has another go.

Dance Class

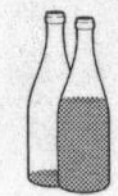

Players: 4-10

This is a 'must' for all those who sew their own sequins and are devotees of *Come Dancing*. Prepare a list of dances – tango, waltz, rumba, charleston, twist, bossa nova, military two-step etc – and ask each player in turn to mime a particular dance. This must be done solo with an imaginary partner. The other players must try to guess the name of the dance. Anyone who has only ever shuffled around a handbag should sit this one out.

As The Word Decrees

Players: Any number

While one person leaves the room, the remainder think of an adverb to be discovered upon his or her return. The single player attempts to find the adverb by asking the others to perform mimes 'as the word decrees'. For example, he or she might say: 'Open a can of baked beans as the word decrees.' Depending upon the adverb, that player will then mime the opening of the tin passionately, slowly, breathlessly, dreamily, artistically, deviously, majestically, nervously, solemnly, ineptly, violently, athletically and so on. If the single player is unable to work out the adverb from that mime, he or she may ask someone else to do a different mime – say, hammering a nail — as the word decrees. A total of four mimes are permitted. If the adverb has not been deduced by then, a forfeit must be paid and another player is sent from the room.

Speech Patterns

Players: 3 or more

This game is best played by groups of three who must conduct impromptu conversations in which the first letter of the first word of a sentence must be the same as the last letter of the last word of the previous speaker's sentence. Thus player one might begin: 'What shall we do today, Max?' And player two might reply: 'Xylophones! We'll get out the xylophones and play some jazz.' This puts player three in something of a predicament until he or she exclaims: 'Zounds! What a great idea.' And the game continues in strict rotation and alphabetical sequence with each player trying to drop the next one into the mire. Anyone who fails to think of an answer within 10 seconds, or whose answer is adjudged to bear no relation whatsoever to the conversation, is eliminated. When the first group are reduced to one, the next trio can have a go.

Inquisition

Players: 3 or more

As with 'Speech Patterns', this game is best played in groups of three. Once again, the intention is for the players to hold a reasonably meaningful conversation but this time they can only speak in questions. Each question must be answered with another question. Anyone who gives a reply that is not a question is eliminated. The longer this game goes on, the more irritating it can become as every attempt to induce a statement is parried. In the circumstances it is advisable not to team up players of a volatile nature lest the proceedings degenerate into a brawl.

Mimics

Players: Any number

Before the party, draw up a list of famous people (dead or alive, real or fictional) with distinctive voices. Assign a celebrity to each player and ask them, in turn, to read out a short newspaper cutting in the voice of their chosen character. The other players then have to guess who is being impersonated. There are no winners, but who cares?

Tableaux

Players: 6 or more

You will need:
A selection of old clothes

If you've got a pile of old clothes waiting to go out for jumble, use them first as the costumes for this entertaining still life game. With the players divided into teams, the first team dress up to depict a film, a book, a painting or even a scene from history such as Drake playing bowls while waiting for the Armada. The actors are not allowed to speak and must stand absolutely still either for a minute or until the other team guesses the subject matter correctly. If the title is not guessed within the time limit, the losing team must pay a forfeit. If it is guessed, the next team have a go. Unless you have a particularly large number of guests you should avoid attempting a scene from *Ben Hur*.

Paper Costumes

Players: Any number

You will need:
A supply of newspapers, pins

Would-be Vivienne Westwoods can try their luck at designing something for the catwalk, using nothing more than the obituary column of *The Daily Telegraph* and the sports pages of *The Sun*. Each player is given 15 minutes to create a little number from a stack of newspapers which can be held in place by pins. Then they have to model it in front of their adoring audience who must to try to guess what on earth it's supposed to be — that is, provided the creator knows what it's meant to be themselves. Prizes can be awarded for the player who comes up with the most imaginative outfit as well as for the best model.

Lateral Thinking

Players: 4-8

You will need:
Pencil and paper

One player thinks up a beginning, a middle and an end for a short play. This can be either dialogue or actions. The others then have 10 minutes to build a playlet around the set pieces, at the end of which they must perform it. A suitable framework might be:

> Beginning: 'Clive, it's the first time I've seen you since your sex-change operation went so horribly wrong.'
> Middle: The gun fell to the floor with a resounding thud.
> End: And she never ate anchovies again.

Five-Minute Theatre

Players: 4-10

You will need:
Pencils and paper, pieces of card

In advance, write lines of dialogue (one per player) on separate pieces of card. Each player then picks a card and has five minutes to pen a script ending with the given line. The finished articles are then read out, the most ingenious story being declared the winner. Here are a few possible closing lines:

Thank goodness Mrs. Jenkins is a black belt in karate!'
'That's the last time I wear red nail varnish.'
'Phew! I thought that killer iguana was going to wipe us all out.'
'Who'd have thought trainspotting could be so exciting!'
'Anyone for porridge?'

My Name Is...

Players: 3-10

One player leaves the room and the rest think of a famous person. When the player returns, he or she is allowed to ask each of the others two questions in an effort to establish the identity. The questions can only be answered by 'yes' or 'no'. When the interrogation is complete, the player must do an impression of whoever he or she thinks it is. Poor questioning can lead to hapless individuals doing an impersonation of Boadicea when they're supposed to be Fanny Craddock. But then again, it's an easy mistake to make.

What's the Use?

Players: 5-10

You will need:
Various unusual objects

This is a quick-fire improvisation game whereby each player is given a strange-looking object (such as a sink plunger, a boomerang or a pair of cycle clips) and asked to think of as many amusing uses for it as possible. The one who comes up with the most ideas is the winner.

Paranoia

Players: Any number

While one person is out of the room, the other players decide on a common factor which will dictate all their answers when he or she returns. By asking endless questions, the player has to work out what that factor is. They may choose to be cannibals, to end every sentence in a preposition or to treat the questioner as if he or she has an unpleasant social disease. Or, of course, they may drive the questioner to the brink of insanity by all pretending to be hard of hearing, in which case the game can go on and on indefinitely.

Drama School

Players: 5-10

Impotence, frustration and anger. Besides being three emotions which occur on a daily basis among passengers on the London Underground, these are also prime examples of moods which players might be called upon to express in 'Drama School'. One player acts as judge and gives the others a range of emotions to convey, such as lust, panic, guilt, boredom and terror. A point is awarded to the player who gives the most convincing demonstration of each feeling, the winner being the one with the highest total at the end of the game. All of the actions should be silent and the game is even more rewarding if the players have to rely solely on facial expressions with no hand gestures allowed.

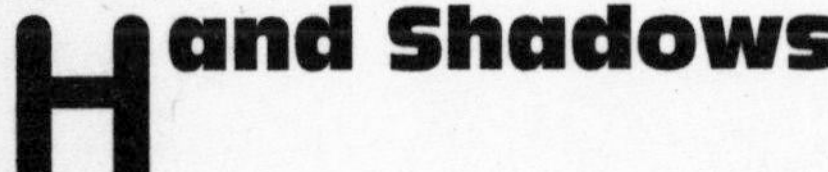

Hand Shadows

Players: 5-10

You will need:
A white sheet or a screen of white paper, a lamp, pieces of paper, a hat or bowl

Two guests hold a white sheet or screen of white paper at either end. A lamp is placed behind the screen. The names of various animals are written down on separate slips of paper and put into a hat or bowl. One by one, the players draw a slip and, using their hands only, must cast a shadow of the named creature onto the screen. The best results are achieved by standing at the side of the screen. While rabbit, dog and horse are fairly straightforward, the poor player who draws millipede may need to enlist a little help.

Just a Minute

Players: 4-8

A popular Victorian parlour game, 'Just a Minute' has long been a mainstay of BBC Radio 4. Each player is given a topic by the referee and told to speak about it for a minute without hesitating, straying from the subject or being guilty of repetition. Any of the other players who spot one of the aforementioned sins may challenge the speaker, at which point the clock is stopped while the arguments rage. If the challenge is upheld by the umpire, the challenger earns a point and speaks on the same subject for what is left of the original minute. If the challenge is rejected, the first speaker gains a point and resumes from where he or she was so rudely interrupted. Whoever is speaking at the end of the minute scores a point or two points if it is still the original speaker. The following topics may prove suitable for earnest discussion:

Mud
The house fly
The Battle of Cropredy Bridge (1643)
Underarm hair
Semolina
The life and times of Arthur Mullard

Fairy Tales

Players: Any number

Players are divided into two teams to act out improvised versions of well-known fairy tales, but as famous people rather than themselves. Thus, Little Red Riding Hood might feature Waynetta Slob as *Red Riding Hood*, Julian Clary as the Wolf and Tommy Cooper as the Woodcutter. At the end of each performance, the other team has to guess the fairy story and the double identity of all of the players. If you are blessed with a particularly artistic gathering, you may choose to have the play acted in the style of a famous film director. Quentin Tarantino's version of *Cinderella* where the Fairy Godmother turns out to be a serial killer and Buttons dies in a gangland shoot-out invariably proves popular.

Scene and Heard

Players: 8 or more

You will need:
Pencils and paper

Each woman is supplied with a pencil, a paper and a man. Together they then compose the first scene of a film — it could be a farce, a murder mystery, a sci-fi extravaganza, a musical, anything. After five minutes, each of the men move round one so that the first man teams up with the second woman and works with her on the second scene of her scenario. After a further five minutes, he moves on to a third woman and helps with her third scene. The cycle continues until every woman has written one scene with every man. At the end, the screenplays are acted out and a vote is taken as to which is the most entertaining.

Strictly for Posers

Players: Any number

You will need:
Pieces of paper, a hat or bowl

Write down a selection of adjectives – such as tragic, gobsmacked or amorous – on separate slips of paper and put them into a hat or some other container. Each player draws a slip from the container and has to strike a pose which captures the selected word. The others then have to guess the adjective.

Telly Favourites

Players: 8 or more

Divide the players into two groups and ask three or four members of each group to act out a scenario from a TV series of their choice, anything from *Casualty* to *Postman Pat*. In doing so, they must not use any character names. At the end of the performance, which should not exceed two minutes, the other members of their team have to try to guess the name of the programme. If they fail to do so in three guesses, the second team are allowed a guess. Then the second team perform their scenario.

Romeo and Juliet

Players: Any even number

A man and a woman leave the room and the remainder think up identities for them to assume on their return. Each is told individually whom they are to be. They then have to woo each other intently for five minutes, at the end of which they must try to guess their suitor's identity. When thinking of pairs of names, try to come up with unlikely lovers such as Rambo and Bonnie Langford, Compo from *Last of the Summer Wine* and Joan Collins, Henry VIII and Mavis from *Coronation Street*, or Madonna and Rin Tin Tin.

Party Guests

Players: 4-8

One player acts as the host while the others are given secret identities, the more unusual the better. By studying what these 'guests' say and do when they arrive at the party, the host has to work out who or what each one is supposed to be. The only question the host is allowed to ask is the guess itself — for example: 'Are you a dyslexic signwriter?' If the answer is 'yes', the host moves on to the next guest. The game ends when the host has identified all of the guests. Here are some suggestions for your guest list:

Scrupulously honest second-hand car dealer
End of pier entertainer
Nun-turned-glamour model
Grave digger
Politically correct plumber.
Tina Turner
Incontinent jockey

TAKING A BREATHER

Printer's Errors

Players: Any number

You will need:
Newspapers or magazines

Cut out 10-line passages from newspapers or magazines, one passage per player. Then cut the passages into individual lines and rearrange them so that they make no sense whatsoever. (This stage can be skipped with *The Guardian*.) The players then have to repair their section of print so that the lines are in the correct order, the first to do so being the winner.

Suitcases

Players: Any number

In this memory game, players have to recite an ever-lengthening list of strange items, supposedly the contents of a suitcase for a month abroad at an exotic destination. The players sit in a circle and the first may announce: 'I packed my suitcase and in it I put 36 back issues of *Reader's Digest*.' Then player two might say: 'I packed my suitcase and in it I put 36 back issues of *Reader's Digest* and a *Tom and Jerry* alarm clock with fluorescent numerals.' The burden then passes to the third player who may reveal: 'I packed my suitcase and in it I put 36 back issues of *Reader's Digest*, a *Tom and Jerry* alarm clock with fluorescent numerals and a size 10 black, frilly, lacy negligee from British Home Stores, Dagenham branch.' And so it continues, with anybody who forgets an item or gets it in the wrong order being obliged to drop out. The game ends when there is only one-word perfect suitcase packer left.

Taboo

Players: Any number

Pick a letter from the alphabet and declare that nobody is allowed to use a word containing that letter. Then ask each player in turn a question, cunningly designed to catch them out. If the forbidden letter is 'L', you may choose to ask: 'What is the capital of England?' Unable to say 'London' because it contains an 'L', a quick-thinking player may reply: 'The city on the River Thames'. As the questioning becomes more intense, any player who slips up and uses the taboo letter is eliminated. The last player left answering questions is the winner.

Rhyming Time

Players: Any number

You will need:
Pencils and paper, a hat or bowl

Every player writes down his or her name and a simple word on a piece of paper and then puts the slip in a hat. One of the group acts as umpire and draws a slip, telling the person whose name it bears not to take part because that person knows the mystery word. The umpire then gives the other players a word which rhymes with the word on the piece of paper. If the word on the paper is 'night', the umpire may reveal that the word rhymes with 'tight'. Armed with this information, the remaining players try to guess the mystery word by asking a series of questions, whereupon the umpire must reply using the word being suggested. Thus 'Is it violent?' would be answered with 'No, it's not fight' and 'Is it the opposite to dark?' with 'No, it's not light'. The game ends when someone finally discovers the word.

Sausages!

Players: Any number

Here, players bombard a chosen victim with two minutes of questions, to which the reply must always be 'sausages!' The interrogators tailor their questions in the hope of inducing the victim to crack up when answering 'sausages!' as the key rule of the game is that the respondent must keep a straight face at all times. If he or she fails to do so, the game is over and a new victim is selected. It may sound easy, but earnestly answering 'sausages!' is no mean feat with questions such as: 'What do you clean your ears with?' and 'What are baby pigs called?'

Mystery Tour

Players: Any number

While one player leaves the room, the rest choose a country to where he or she is to pay an imaginary visit. On his return, the selected player asks the other players in turn: 'Where am I going?' Each player gives a different minor clue, such as Frida Boccara represented this country in the 1969 Eurovision Song Contest, the aim being to prevent the questioner from discovering the destination. When the country has been correctly identified, another player has a go — unless of course it took so long that everyone has gone home. In case you wondered, Frida Boccara represented France and was the joint winner with a catchy little ditty entitled *Un Jour, Un Enfant*.

Word Association

Players: Any number

Always a hit at psychiatrists' parties, 'Word Association' requires the players to sit in a circle. The first player says the first word that comes into his or her head. The second player immediately says the first word he or she can think of in response to the first player's word and so the quick-fire patter continues around the circle. Anyone who hesitates is eliminated. The game can, of course, reveal a number of secrets better left hidden so if the previous player says 'breasts', beware of blurting out the name of anyone other than your partner.

Compounds

Players: Any number

The first player calls out a two-word compound, such as 'washout', and succeeding players have to think up a corresponding compound in so far as the first half of the word is the same as that of the second part of the previous word. Thus 'washout' could be followed by 'outhouse', 'house mouse', 'mousetrap', 'trapdoor', 'doorstop', 'stopover', 'overarm', 'armrest' and so on. Anyone unable to find a continuation may claim that none is possible. If the claim is upheld, the previous player (the one who supplied the word) is eliminated and the challenger starts a new round. If, however, someone does think of a valid word, the challenger has to drop out.

Predicaments

Players: Any number

Life has a nasty habit of placing us in awkward predicaments, so this game may prove invaluable should you ever find yourself stuck in a lift with the world farting champion, attending a police identity parade in a heavily bloodstained shirt or turning up at a party dressed as King Canute when everyone else is in suit and tie. One player is sent from the room while the others choose an embarrassing situation in which to place him or her. When that person returns, he or she asks each of the other players in turn what they would do in certain circumstances, presenting different situations to each one. Totally disregarding the subject matter of the question, they instead have to give answers which relate to a completely different predicament which they have devised. From these answers, the person has to work out the precise nature of the chosen predicament. The game can create a succession of splendid non-sequiteurs. If the agreed predicament is that the questioner, a keen naturalist, accidentally enrolled in a naturists' weekend, the question: 'What would you do if you got your finger stuck in the teapot spout?' could prompt replies ranging from: 'Pray that the weather stayed nice' to 'Shake hands very carefully' or 'Just turn the other cheek'.

Spelling Bee

Players: Any number

One player assumes the role of question master and asks the other players in turn to spell a series of words. Any player who gets a spelling wrong is eliminated. The winner is the last one left in. It is best to start with moderately easy words and then make the spellings progressively tougher as the rounds progress.

Backward Spelling

Players: Any number

The rules are the same as for 'Spelling Bee' except that here the players are presented with the additional problem that all of the words have to be spelt backwards.

Intruders

Players: Any number

For this sophisticated version of 'Odd One Out', you need to prepare a list of at least 20 items which belong to the same category plus one which doesn't. If you read out Aire, Calder, Waveney, Esk, Cuckmere, Mole, Ouse, Trent, Rother, Fowey, Exe, Tees, Test, Taff, Nene, Itchen, Ribble, Eden, Thames, Avon and Don, the winner of that round will be the first person who calls out 'Taff'. That's because it is a Welsh river and the rest are English. Other likely categories could be FA Cup-winning teams (slipping in one club which has never won the Cup), Nobel prize winners (plus one who didn't) and number one hit songs (with one that wasn't).

Common Factors

Players: Any number

Prepare a series of lists, each comprising three seemingly unconnected people or objects but which do actually have something in common. The first person to call out the common factor wins absolutely nothing except the undying admiration of his peers. An example is 'Australian fast bowler, Gnasher and the London Fire Brigade', the connection being Dennis — Dennis Lillee, Dennis the Menace and fire engines are made by Dennis. The more obscure you can make the link, the more fun you'll have as your guests flounder around aimlessly.

Call My Bluff

Players: 5-10

The popular TV game can be equally successful at a party. Beforehand, sift through the pages of a dictionary and pick out a dozen or so obscure words. In addition to the correct definition, think of four additional bogus definitions for each word. Announce the first word, making sure to spell it out to the players and pronounce it correctly, and then read out the five definitions. Each player is then asked to say which he or she thinks is the correct meaning. A point is scored for each right answer.

Song Titles

Players: Any number

Think of a word which occurs frequently in song titles – 'love', 'blue', 'you' etc. Going round the room, ask each player to think of a song title featuring the chosen word. Anyone who fails to come up with an answer has to drop out. And if you only want a very short game, try 'supercalifragilisticexpialidocious' as the keyword.

Buzz

Players: Any number

For maximum enjoyment, this game should be played as speedily as possible with no hesitation en route. The players sit in a circle. The first player calls out 'One', the next player 'Two', the next 'Three' and so on. When the number seven or any multiple of seven is reached, the players must call out 'Buzz'. If the number contains a seven, but is not a multiple of it, only part of it is replaced by 'Buzz'. Thus 71 would be 'Buzzty-one' and 37 'Thirty-Buzz'. If a player forgets to say 'Buzz' or hesitates too long, he or she drops out. The last player to stay in the game is the winner. A variation on this game is 'Fizz'. It is played in exactly the same way as 'Buzz' except that the magical number is five. Thus 50 is 'Fizzty'.

Buzz-Fizz

Players: Any number

Mayhem reigns supreme in this combination of 'Buzz' and 'Fizz' in which 75 becomes 'Buzzty-Fizz' and 57 'Fizzty-Buzz'. Anyone who buzzes when he should be fizzing is consigned to the sidelines. To make things more interesting, try switching games mid-way through from 'Buzz' or 'Fizz' to 'Buzz-Fizz'.

Mini Words

Players: Any number

For this game, you need to think of some eight-letter words which also contain anagrams of one three, one four and one five-letter word. For example, 'treasure' contains 'ear', 'rust' and 'erase'. It is important that these mini words use up all of the letters in the big word. First you give the players the three-letter word and invite them to guess the eight-letter word from that clue. Any correct deduction at this stage earns three points. If there are no takers, you give the four-letter clue, a successful guess at which earns two points. Finally you give them the five-letter clue which is worth one point. If the eight-letter word still remains unsolved, put them out of their misery and move on to the next word... or suggest something rather less intellectually demanding — like a nice easy game of musical chairs perhaps.

Up Jenkins!

Players: 6-10

You will need:
A coin, table and chairs

For this classic game of bluff, counter-bluff and counter-counter-bluff, the players sit as two teams on opposite sides of the table. The members of one team conceal their hands below the table and pass a coin along the row from hand to hand. When the leader of the other team shouts out 'Up Jenkins!' the players on the team with the coin must raise their hands, with fists clenched, well above the table. The opposing leader then commands 'Down Jenkins!' at which the raised hands must be slapped down onto the table, palms flat, as hard as possible to mask the sound of the coin hitting the table. The opposing team must now guess which hand the coin is under. This is where players with empty hands will deliberately mislead and behave is if they have the coin. After lengthy consultation, a verdict is reached and the leader taps the chosen hand. If it does contain the coin, the guessing team score a point; if not, the point goes to the team with the coin. After each round, the two teams swap roles.

Sandwiches

Players: Any number

Seat the players in a circle and pluck a fairly common letter from the alphabet. Tell them that, going round in turn, they have to try to think of a word beginning and ending with that letter. For instance, if the chosen letter was A, words might include 'Australia, algebra, aurora, Austria, arena, Antarctica, ambrosia (not the creamed rice), auricula, aurelia, Argentina, aureola, acacia and Asia'. However, 'Abba' would not be permitted. Players score a point for each correct word. When everyone feels that one letter has been exhausted, move on to another letter, but don't make it something like J, unless you are

in a hurry to go and make the coffee. The player with the highest total is declared the master wordsmith.

Jackanory

Players: Any number

You will need:
A stop-watch

The players should sit in a circle with their legs intertwined. Those with an aversion to the person sitting next to them should either sit elsewhere or settle for touching knees. One player begins a story on any subject and must talk for 30 seconds without hesitation or repetition. The time is kept by a stopwatch-wielding judge who, at the end of the 30 seconds, calls 'Time up' and the story must then be continued from precisely where it left off (often in mid-sentence) by the next player. The 30-second stories continue round the circle with the judge watching for long pauses, repetition or anyone who makes the mistake of ending the story. Any player who is guilty of these deeds is promptly eliminated. The winner is the last player left talking.

The Smelling Game

Players: Any number

You will need:
Various items with distinctive smells, saucers, cloths, blindfolds, pencils and paper

Place a selection of strong-smelling items in separate saucers and cover each one with a cloth. The blindfolded players pass along the row and endeavour to identify the assorted scents, writing down their answers on a piece of paper. A suitably pungent grouping might be: turpentine, lavender, crushed garlic, boot polish, sage, bleach, thyme, tobacco and raw egg. Players should be warned that they remove the cloth covering the saucer at their peril.

Balloon Roll

Players: Any even number

You will need:
Balloons

Since even the most sloth-like individual would be hard pushed to describe this balloon game as an athletic pursuit, it has made its way into these gentler offerings. The players are split into pairs and each pair is given a balloon. They stand facing each other with the balloon wedged between them at waist height. No hands may be used, the balloon being held in place solely by body pressure. Each pair have to turn three complete circles on the spot while keeping the balloon between them. If a balloon is dropped, it may be picked up by hand but it also negates one turn. Any couple who burst their balloon are automatically disqualified.

Traveller's Alphabet

Players: Any number

With all participants seated in a circle, the first player turns to the person on his or her left and asks: 'Where are you going?' The second player must think of a destination beginning with an A. The first player then asks: 'And what will you do there?' whereupon the second player must reply using a verb, an adjective and a noun, all beginning with the letter A. If the destination is Argentina, the activity might be 'assessing Argentinian armadillos'. The second player then asks the same questions of the third player whose answers must all start with B. And so the game continues round the room with whoever is due to get Q breaking out in beads of perspiration. Any player who cannot come up with suitable answers is knocked out of the game, the winner being the last one left in.

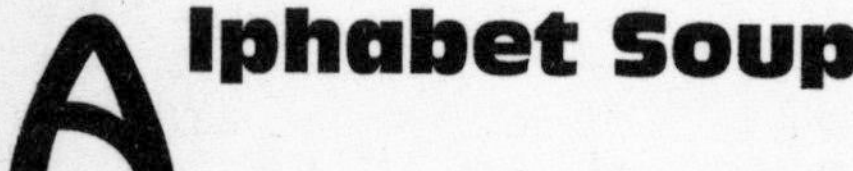

Alphabet Soup

Players: Any number

For this alphabet game, the players should again sit in a circle. The first player announces: 'I went to a banquet' and thinks of a food beginning with A to eat — anchovies, apples etc. The second player has to do the same with B, so that he or she might say: 'I went to a banquet and ate anchovies and beetroot.' And so the game continues with a little sprinkling of custard, dates, eggs, fish fingers, gooseberries right up until the poor soul who faces a meal of zebra. It is probably best not to play 'Alphabet Soup' on a full stomach.

Hypochondriac

Players: Any number

The rules here are the same as for 'Alphabet Soup' except that the subject matter is illness and disease instead of food. The first player might declare, 'I went into hospital because I had athlete's foot.' Soon one unfortunate will be revealing a medical history consisting of athlete's foot, boils, colic, dysentery, earache, foot and mouth disease, gangrene and hard pad.'

Matchmaker

Players: Any number

You will need:
An empty wine bottle, a supply of matches

This game requires the steadiest of hands and is therefore best played before too much alcohol has been consumed. Four matches are placed across the mouth of an empty wine bottle and players then take it turns to add a match at a time, the aim being to build up a mountain of sticks. There are no winners, but the player whose clumsiness causes the construction to collapse must pay a suitable forfeit.

Chinese Whispers

Players: Any number

Usually played over a garden fence, this old favourite is the ultimate treat for local gossips. Everyone sits in a circle and the first player invents an item of gossip which is whispered once only to the person on his or her right. The morsel of information continues its journey around the room in this way until it arrives back with the originator who then reads out the first and last messages. Unless your guests are trained listeners, the end product invariably bears little relation to the original. An opening rumour of 'Ron's seeing Pam from the chip shop' will quickly be distorted to 'Don eats Spam in flip-flops' and may well end up as 'Last night I dreamt I went to Manderley again'.

Likes and Dislikes

Players: Any number

Thought to be a favourite of Frances Hodgson-Burnett, author of *Little Lord Fauntleroy*, this game requires the utmost attention from participants. One player reads out a list of likes and dislikes, all of which have a common theme. The others have to listen intently and try to spot the link. The first person to do so wins the round. Here is an example:

I like roses, but I don't like carnations
I like wood, but I don't like timber
I like fish, but I don't like chips
I like biscuits, but I don't like cakes
I like collars, but I don't like ties

The answer here is that all of the likes can be prefaced by 'dog' (dog roses, dogwood, dogfish, dog biscuits, dog collars) whereas the dislikes can't.

Concentration

Players: 4-8

You will need:
A pack of playing cards

An excellent test of memory, Concentration is played with a full pack of playing cards which are shuffled and placed face down on a table. Each player in turn selects two cards and turns them face upwards. The aim is to find two of a kind (threes, jacks, nines, aces etc) and when that happens, those two cards are removed from the table and placed next to the successful player who then has another turn. That player's turn continues until he or she fails to produce a match, at which point the cards are put back face down in the same positions. The winner is the player with most pairs when all 52 cards have been claimed.

Shadows

Players: Any number

You will need:
A white sheet, a lamp, a variety of small objects

Hang a sheet in such a way that sufficient light is cast on it to produce a good shadow. From behind the sheet, hold a series of everyday items at such angles that their shadows make it difficult for the players in front to recognise. When doing this, you should try to keep your hand as much out of the way as possible for fear of confusing everyone still further. The first person to identify each object correctly earns a point. Items you could use include an alarm clock, a plug, a cotton reel, a corkscrew, nutcrackers, an eggcup and a light bulb.

Botticelli

Players: Any number

Taking its name from the 15th-century Italian artist — even though it is highly doubtful whether he ever actually played it, at least not with a bowl of Twiglets in one hand — 'Botticelli' is a devious question and answer game. It starts with one player thinking of the name of a famous person (dead or alive, real or fictional) and announcing the first letter of the subject's surname to the assembled throng. They then have to bombard the player with a succession of indirect questions. If the mystery person is Samson and the letter is therefore S, they may ask: 'Are you a former leader of the Liberal party?' to which the player will reply: 'No I am not Sir David Steel.' They may try: 'Are you a cigar-smoking disc jockey?' to which the player will reply: 'No, I am not Sir Jimmy Savile OBE.' Trying to make each question more difficult, they may ask: 'Did you produce The Crystals?' in the hope that the player will be unable to come up with Phil Spector. If the player can't answer a question, the others are allowed to ask one direct question such as 'Are you alive?' or 'Are you male?' By engineering as many direct questions as possible, they should eventually arrive at Samson, but even then they can only seek confirmation of the fact once they have earned the right to ask a direct question.

Initial Questions

Players: Any number

Devise a series of questions which offer plenty of scope for the imagination, such as: 'What is your favourite food?', 'What is your pet hate?' or 'What turns you on?' Each player in turn has to come up with an answer, the words of which must begin with his or her initials. Thus Mildred Winona Beryl Edison might list as her favourite food '**M**uesli **W**ith **B**oiled **E**lderberries', her pet hate as '**M**en **W**ith **B**ushy **E**yebrows' and confess that she gets turned on by '**M**en **W**ho **B**ruise **E**asily'.

Train of Thought

Players: 4-8

This form of word association has an unexpected sting in the tail. The first player thinks of a word (perhaps 'kettle') and the rest in turn think of the first word that comes into their mind. When each player has had three turns (so that with eight players there would be 24 words in the chain), the next player has to rewind it, recalling each word in the correct reverse order right back to the start. If a player makes a mistake, it passes to the next in line. Whoever completes the rewinding process by announcing 'kettle' or whatever, wins the game.

The Minister's Cat

Players: Any number

The first player thinks of an adjective beginning with 'A' such as 'aggressive' and declares: 'The Minister's Cat is aggressive'. The next player adds an appropriate adjective beginning with a B and subsequent players must repeat all the adjectives used after adding their own. Soon we learn that the Minister's Cat is 'zealous, youthful, xenophobic, wily, vengeful, uncouth, treacherous, spiteful, round, quixotic, promiscuous, odd, noisy, miserable, lethal, knowing, jumping, ignorant, healthy, ginger, fierce, erudite, devious, calculating, bombastic and aggressive.' When Z is reached, the players go back to A and start again.

Converse in Verse

Players: Any number

This is a good game to play after a few drinks. All of the participants must talk in verse, anyone who slips up being obliged to pay a forfeit. It may take a while to warm up but once everyone has got the hang of it, they'll be chatting away in rhymes as if it was the most natural thing in the world to do... and probably long after the game has finished.

Mismatches

Players: Any even number

The players divide into two teams and study the lounge for 30 seconds. While one team leaves the room, the other has two minutes in which to make a number of minor alterations to the room — moving a vase, placing a different magazine at the top of the pile. Wholesale redecorating is not recommended, neither is emptying the water from the goldfish bowl. At the end of the two minutes, the absentees return and attempt to spot the changes. One point is scored for each correctly-spotted mismatch, the other team gaining a point for each one that goes unnoticed. Then the two teams swap roles.

The Atlas Game

Players: 8-12

This game should not be attempted by anyone who scored lower than a grade D at GCSE geography. One player is sent from the room while the others decide upon the name of a town which the missing player must identify from a series of cunning clues. The town selected should have the same number of letters as there are players left in the room — say SCUNTHORPE for 10 players. Each letter of the town is assigned to a different player who must then think of another town beginning with that letter. It is this second town which will yield the clue. The questioner returns and says to the player with the first letter of the mystery town: 'Tell me something about your town.' The player with the S has thought of Sydney as the alternative and gives four clues relating to Sydney — famous cricket ground, heavy lager drinkers, big bridge, opera house. When the questioner has deduced that the town being described is Sydney, he or she will know that the first letter of the sought-after word is an S. The game continues in this way through the remainder of the letters. If the questioner is unable to detect any town being described, he or she is left with a blank space and must hope to solve the riddle from the other letters. You'll probably find that one round of this game is quite sufficient.

The Yes, No Interlude

Players: 5-10

Fans of the TV game show *Take Your Pick* (and there must be some) will revel in the opportunity to re-create the infamous 'Yes, No Interlude'. One person is appointed question master and the remaining players are then wheeled in individually and subjected to intense questioning, during which they must refrain from using the words 'Yes' or 'No'. The player who keeps going the longest is the winner. If this exceeds 10 minutes, give it up as a lost cause and move on to the next player.

Initial Help

Players: Any number

The first player thinks of a letter in the alphabet, say H, and gives a clue to a three-letter word beginning with that letter, as in 'H plus two letters is what you make while the sun shines' (hay).Whoever guesses correctly then thinks up a clue for a four-letter word beginning with H and so it goes on with the words getting progressively longer. When you can't think of a 15-letter word starting with H, move on to another letter. Finish the game when terminal boredom has set in.

Anagram Action

Players: 6 or more

Prepare a series of anagrams of seven letters or more and, with the players seated attentively, read out slowly and steadily the letters of the first anagram. The first player to call out the correct solution scores a point.

What a Corker!

Players: Any even number

You will need:
10 crown corks

The best thing about this game is that to obtain the equipment necessary to play it, you have to drink 10 bottles of champagne. Once you've sobered up, set the corks in two rows of five, serrated edges down, on opposite sides of a table. Divide the players into two teams and invite one player from each team to try to turn the corks over, using only one finger. This is done by placing the finger on top of the cork and pressing on its edge. When one player has turned over all five, the next team mate takes over in relay fashion. Note: digit dampening is prohibited.

Alpha and Omega

Players: Any number

The players choose a fairly broad category — animals, rock bands, flowers, famous people etc — and the first person calls out any word belonging to the selected category. The second player then calls out another, beginning with the last letter of the first word, and the game continues in this fashion around the room. If the subject was rock bands, it could begin Genesis, Squeeze, Erasure, Eurythmics, Styx, XTC, Chicory Tip, Pulp, Prefab Sprout... Repetition or failure to think of a word results in elimination. The last player left in is the winner.

Rapid Response

Players: Any number

You will need:
Slips of paper, pencils, a hat or bowl

Give each player a pencil and two slips of paper and ask them to write the name of an unlikely object on each slip. All of the slips are shuffled around in a hat or bowl. The person chosen to act as question master draws out two slips at random and asks the first player a question — the dafter the better — the reply to which must mention both objects. For example, if the objects are a pair of Y-Fronts and an Eccles cake and the question is: 'Why do birds suddenly appear, every time you are near?', the reply could be: 'Because they come down for the Eccles cake which I hang up in a pair of your old Y-Fronts.' The person adjudged to have provided the best answer is declared the winner.

Stinkety Pinkety

Players: Any number

One player thinks up a definition, the answer to which is a rhyming adjective and noun. Thus 'a large sow' would be 'a big pig' and 'a metallic garden ornament' would be 'a chrome gnome'. The first player to call out the correct answer gains a point and supplies the next definition. As everyone becomes adept at this pastime, you can move on to rhyming words of more than one syllable such as 'a big cat on an Alpine mountain' (an 'Eiger tiger'), 'university intelligence' ('college knowledge') and 'a furry rodent from Merseyside' (a 'Wirral squirrel').

Cross-examination

Players: Any number

One player, the examiner, is sent from the room while the others decide upon an object or a person. When the examiner returns, he or she has to identify the object by asking four questions: 'Why do you like it?', 'When do you like it?', 'How do you like it?' and 'Where do you like it?' The answers to these questions must be truthful without revealing too much. For instance, if the respective answers were: 'Because it satisfies two people', 'First thing in the morning', 'Warm and moist', and 'Across the kitchen table', it would be an inspired guess to come up with the correct answer of tea bag. The examiner is allowed three guesses which can be made at any time during the questioning. Players take it in turns to act as examiner.

Disassociation

Players: Any number

Here is the opposite to 'Word Association' — a game where each word must bear absolutely no relation to the one before. Anyone who can spot a connection may issue a challenge and if the challenge is upheld by the other players, the challenged player loses a life. The first player to lose three lives brings the game to an end and must pay a forfeit. A sequence beginning 'orange, camel, cannon, lettuce, undertaker, golf ball, xylophone, chimney sweep' might seem totally unconnected but could bring about a challenge because Sooty, whose best friend is Sweep, used to play the xylophone, and might still do for all we know.

Strip Search

Players: 4-8

You will need:
A newspaper

Give each player one sheet from the same-sized newspaper. Starting at the top left-hand corner, they have to tear a continuous strip round and round until they have exhausted their sheet. The player with the longest unbroken strip wins.

Twenty Questions

Players: Any number

Also known as 'Animal, Vegetable, Mineral', this is one of the most popular word games in the world, enjoyed by young and old alike. One person thinks of an object and tells the other players whether it is animal, vegetable, mineral or a combination of two. Humans count as animals, which will come as no surprise to anyone who's ever watched Arsenal play. The others then ask a series of questions, which can only be answered 'Yes' or 'No', in a bid to find the solution. If they succeed before 20 questions have been asked, they win. If not, the single player wins and as a reward is allowed to have another turn.

Wedding Gifts

Players: 5-10

You will need:
Pencils and paper, slips of paper and card

Each player assumes the role of someone who is soon to be married and who has just been presented with a wedding gift by work colleagues. He or she then has to make a thank-you speech, gushing over the joys of the present and how his or her future spouse will also derive enormous pleasure from it, but without ever mentioning it by name. To prepare their short speeches, the players are each given pencil and paper and a slip of paper bearing the name of the present. However, what they don't know is that the shop has accidentally sent an entirely different gift. As they read out their speeches behind a chair, the name of the replacement gift should be placed on a card in front of the chair so that the rest of the players can see it. Only when the speaker has finished does he or she discover the true identity of the gift. The prospective bride who has been eulogising about what she believes to be a sandwich-grill and how it 'cooks beautifully, quickly and evenly' may be rather disturbed to learn that she has been sent a budgie instead.

I Love My Love

Players: Any number

'I love my love with an A', declares player one, 'because she is ambidextrous and acquiesces appealingly. I hate her when she is antagonistic and acts appallingly. I took her to Aberdeen and treated her to anchovies and apricots. Her name is Avril and she comes from Alexandria.' The game moves on to the next player who lists the same topics about his or her love, but with every word beginning with B, and so on through the alphabet. The little speeches should be announced without hesitation, anyone who falters or uses a word unknown to the English language is subjected to a forfeit.

What's the Book?

Players: Any number

Here's a game for literary buffs. Lift a series of 10-line extracts from a wide range of books — from Jane Austen, to *Noddy at the Seaside* to the *Volkswagen Polo User's Handbook* — and read one at a time to your guests. Displaying their artistic acumen, they have to try to guess the title or at least the subject matter. Whoever is judged to be the closest earns a point.

Tate Gallery

Players: Any number

You will need:
A large empty picture frame or rectangle of cardboard

In the centre of a circle of players, one person frames his or her face in an empty picture frame or similar-shaped object for two minutes without making any visible facial movement, other than the occasional blink. Anyone who fails to keep a straight face must hand over the frame to the next person and perform a suitable forfeit.

Ghost

Players: Any number

A game with more aliases than the average *Crimewatch* subject (it's also known as Donkey, Monkey, Wraiths and Chain Letters), this begins with all of the players sitting in a circle. The first player thinks of a word of four or more letters and calls out the first letter. The second player thinks of a word beginning with that letter and calls out the second letter of that word. The third player thinks of a word starting with the first two letters and calls out its third letter. The game progresses with each player trying to stretch the chain of letters and avoid calling out the last letter of a word. Any player who finishes a word loses a life. So if the first five letters are R, A, D, I, S, then the sixth player has no option but to add an H and thus complete a word. Players must always have a valid word in mind when adding a letter. They can be challenged if anyone suspects they have just plucked a letter at random without having any idea of a word. The challenged player must then reveal the word he or she was thinking of. If unable to come up with a valid word, he or she loses a life. But if he or she can declare a proper word, it is the challenger who loses a life. Any player who loses three lives is eliminated, the winner being the last player left in.

Backwards Ghost

Players: Any number

For those whose intellectual capacity knows no limits, try playing 'Ghost' backwards, starting with the last letter of a word and working back towards the beginning. In this case, it is the player who announces the initial letter of the word who loses a life.

Carry On Rhyming

Players: Any number

The players sit in a circle and, in a clockwise direction, conduct a conversation so that the first word of their comment rhymes with the last word of the previous speaker's sentence. Anyone who fails in this task has to drop out. The last player left talking is the winner. A typical discussion might go along these lines:

'Now is the winter of our discontent'
'Bent — Richard III, his back was bent, I think.'
'Drink, don't mind if I do.'
'Sue, I'll fetch a glass in anticipation.'
'Asian Chardonnay, with a bit of luck.'

At this point, discretion is definitely the best part of valour.

One-Minute Wonders

Players: 5-10

Each player has a minute to call out as many words as possible beginning with a pre-selected letter. Proper names are permissible but derivatives are not. So in the case of T, 'talk' is allowed, but not 'talked' or 'talking'. The highest score wins.

Movie Quiz

Players: 6-10

This one's strictly for movie fans. Divide the players into two teams, flick through a film guide and announce the title of an old movie. Then ask the following questions: Who starred in the film? Name three co-stars. When was it released? Who was the director? What was it about? The questions should be open to both teams with a point awarded for each correct answer and at the end of, say, half-a-dozen films, the team with most points is the winner.

Bo-ob

Players: Any number

In this game, players greet each other in the finest big business tradition of initials only. But the initials used are not those of the name of the player being greeted, but the first letters of a four or six-letter word. The reply must be in the form of the letters required to complete a word. For example, Mr. Haddock might say to Mr. C. Bass, 'Good morning, D.A.Z.', to which Mr. Bass could reply, 'Nice to see you, Z.L.E.', making the word DAZZLE. The person doing the greeting must have a proper word in mind – if not, he or she faces elimination. And if the player being greeted does not complete the word within 10 seconds, he or she is also out of the game. The last player left in is the winner.

Ring on a String

Players: Any number

You will need:
A length of string, a ring

The players sit close together in a circle holding a piece of string which is long enough to stretch right around the circle. Threaded onto the string is a small ring. While one player stands in the centre, the ring is moved along the string from player to player, constantly switching direction. The player in the middle has to guess who has the ring at any given time. If he or she is right, the two players swap roles. After three incorrect guesses, another player takes over.

Gallows

Players: 4-6

You will need:
A length of string

The players sit in a circle with the tips of their raised forefingers meeting in the middle. Outside the circle lurks the executioner wielding a noose made of string. He slips the noose around the fingertips and holds up the end of the string. When he suddenly shouts 'Death!' and tugs at the string, the players have to try to whip their fingers away without becoming entrapped. Anyone who is too slow and whose finger gets caught in the noose is deemed executed. The winner is the last player left alive.

Backwords

Players: Any number

Draw up a list of a dozen or so words which you can pronounce backwards, such as 'stink' (knits) or 'bulk' (klub). Call out the backward words and award a point to whoever deciphers each one first.

The Big Match

Players: Any number

You will need:
A large box of matches

Place the matches – 50 or more – in a pile on a table. Each player in turn takes up to six matches from the pile, the player who takes the very last match being the winner.

Teapot

Players: 3-8

'Alf wanted to teapot on the teapot pad, the one to the teapot of his typewriter.' It doesn't make a lot of sense until you realise that 'teapot' is the substitute for 'write' and 'right'. And that is the basis of this game – players have to substitute the word 'teapot' for a chosen word that has more than one meaning or for several words that are pronounced the same but have different meanings. One person leaves the room and the others choose their similar-sounding words. The single player then returns and asks a series of questions which must be answered by sentences featuring 'teapot'. When the questioner knows the word, he or she announces it and it is the turn of the player who provided the last answer to leave the room.

Fortunately Unfortunately

Players: Any number

The players sit in a circle and the first player says a sentence beginning with 'Fortunately'. The next player must then say something beginning with 'Unfortunately' and this process of alternate 'Fortunately' and 'Unfortunately' sentences continues around the circle. Each sentence must make sense and anyone who hesitates unduly or who cannot think of a reply is ruled out. The last player left in is the winner. The key to victory is to try to catch the next person out with as ridiculous a statement as possible.

Rings

Players: 4-8

You will need:
Wire coathangers, rubber rings

Almost an athletic pursuit, this gentle indoor version of quoits requires one coathanger and three rubber rings per pair of players. If you haven't got any proper rings, try sneaking the seals from preserving jars. The game is best played between two pairs at a time. The members of each pair should stand diagonally opposite each other, one with the rings, the other with the upturned hanger, so that the throwers have to lob the rings across each other's path to reach their respective targets — their partner's coathanger hook. Whichever pair gets most rings on the hook wins the game. The hanger holders are allowed to move their hangers to catch wayward shots.

Quotation Rotation

Players: Any number

This distinctly highbrow game begins with the players seated in a circle. In turn, they quote famous quotes at each other from memory, but each quote must contain at least one word of the previous player's quote. Anyone unable to think of a suitable quotation drops out. A similar fate meets any player found guilty of inventing a quotation (for these eventualities, it is best to keep a dictionary of quotations at hand). The last player still quoting is the winner.

Clued Up

Players: 3-6

The quiz-master thinks of a word and reads out a one-word clue as to the identity of that word. If nobody guesses the word, another one-word clue is given, and so on until the puzzle is solved. The other players are each allowed one guess after each clue and whoever is the first to come up with the correct answer takes over as quiz-master for the next round. The initial clues should be difficult and open to all manner of interpretation, but the clues should become progressively easier. For example if the mystery word is 'horse', the clues could go: 'fly, clothes, hair, glue, box, radish, chestnut, foal, stallion, Dobbin.' If nobody has got the answer by then, it's really time they went home.

Collections

Players: 5-10

You will need:

A collection of animal ornaments or cuddly toys, pieces of card

If you seem to have spent most of your life tripping over your children's cuddly bandicoot or fluffy Tasmanian Devil then here, at last, is an opportunity to put them to good use. Arrange a dozen soft animal toys on a table and place a name card beside each one. The imaginary names should be as similar as possible to maximise confusion – William, Willum, Wilhelmina, Wilma. The players are called in and have a minute to memorise the names. The toys and cards are then removed. Following a short interval (possibly while another game is being played), the toys are brought back in one at a time and the players are asked to name them. Whoever is first to call out the correct name gains a point. If your house is a cuddly-toy-free zone, you could always play the game with china animals.

I Spy

Players: Any number

Beloved by children, 'I Spy' is nevertheless a nice restful game for a party where everyone has already done too much rushing about. The rules are simple. One player thinks of an object that is visible in the room (say, a cobweb) and says: 'I spy with my little eye something beginning with C.' The other players then have to guess what the object is. The first to guess the word correctly takes over as spy... while the hostess swiftly fetches the dustpan and brush.

Stepping Stones

Players: 3-8

You will need:
Pencils and paper

The degree of intelligence required for this game depends upon the attitude of the participants. The players have to give one of their number a journey from one subject to another via three stepping stones. Up to nine statements may be used to link the five subjects which must be covered in the order given. If a player is told to get from the Royal Family to Tennis via TV, America and Music, here is how the journey could be accomplished:

The Queen lives at Windsor Castle. (Royal Family)
Vic Windsor is a character in *Emmerdale*. (TV)
Barbara Windsor has appeared in a number of *Carry On* films.
The most recent *Carry On* film was *Carry On Columbus*. (America)
It starred Bernard Cribbins who had a hit in the 1960s with *Right Said Fred*. (Music)
Bernard Cribbins narrated *The Wombles* who live on Wimbledon Common. (Tennis)

If on the other hand the 'Stepping Stones' journey is from Nuclear Physics to

Greek Literature via Latin Irregular Verbs, Wagnerian Works and the work of the Pre-Raphaelites, then you're probably at the wrong party.

Deliberate Mistakes

Players: 4-8

Prepare a short story containing a number of factual errors, some obvious, others less so. For example, while most people will know that Nelson didn't fight at Waterloo, how many will remember, or perhaps care, which arm he lost? The story is then read aloud to the players who shout out 'Wrong!' whenever they suspect a mistake. If it is an error, that player gains a point. But an unsuccessful interruption loses a point.

My Old Granny

Players: 5-10

The object of this exercise is simply to make people laugh by uttering ridiculous statements — the sort of thing railway station announcers have been doing for years. The game leader goes to each player in turn and, looking them squarely in the eye, wails plaintively: 'Alas, alas, my old granny spontaneously combusted at bingo last night and I don't know what to do.' In reply, each player must make a reasonable suggestion while maintaining an inscrutably straight face. Anyone caught displaying the slightest hint of mirth will be disqualified. Those remaining take part in round two where the leader enlarges the problem. 'Alas, alas, my old granny spontaneously combusted at bingo last night and Mrs. Jenkins next door has got a banana stuck in her ear and I don't know what to do.' After further helpful suggestions, any straight-faced survivors progress to the third and final round where the leader's dilemma reaches crisis point. 'Alas, alas, my old granny spontaneously combusted at bingo last night and Mrs. Jenkins next door has got a banana stuck in her ear and my boomerang won't come back and I don't know what to

do.' Again suggestions are offered and any player who makes it through all three rounds should receive a prize.

Twin Speakers

Players: Any even number

The players are divided into pairs, each of whom are secretly given connected identities — such as postmaster and postmistress, Pinky and Perky, snakes and ladders, cheese and onion, Sodom and Gomorrah. The first pair (maybe gin and tonic) step forward and the rest of the throng ask a series of questions of both partners. Each query is answerable only by a 'Yes' or 'No'. Whichever pair guesses the identities of the mystery couple will then take their place.

Secret Letter

Players: 5-10

This is a bit like the game 'Taboo' except that here the players don't know the forbidden letter. The questioner picks a secret letter and asks each player in turn a question requiring a one-word answer. If the answer contains the letter, that player loses a life. The first to lose three lives has to pay a forfeit.

Which Word?

Players: Any number

You will need:
Pencil and paper

Another variation of 'Taboo' but this time the forbidden fruit is a word rather than a letter. One person secretly writes the mystery word on a piece of paper and fires questions at each player in turn — the questions are cunningly designed to elicit a reply containing the banned word. For instance if the word is 'duck', questions might include:

'What would you do if a low-flying pigeon came towards you?'
'What's your favourite Chinese dish?'
'What do you see on the lake at the park?'
'What's the lowest score a batsman can get at cricket?'

All answers must be adequate, any player who is deliberately evasive, hesitant or who utters the forbidden word is eliminated. The last one left in is the winner.

MUSICAL INTERLUDES

Musical Statues

Players: Any number

You will need:
Music

This children's favourite can be equally entertaining with adults, particularly those blessed with no sense of rhythm or balance. The players dance away to the music and must be sure to move around rather than just jig on the spot. So even old Aunt Bertha must try a few steps to the sounds of Bon Jovi. When the music stops, everyone must 'freeze' and remain in that position. Any couple choosing to perform the literal version of 'Je t'aime...' could find this command quite pleasurable. Meanwhile, the host or hostess glide around the statues trying to make them move or giggle, but without actually touching them. Anyone who falls victim to their tactics is eliminated. After 20 seconds, the music re-starts and the next round begins. The game continues until only one dancer remains.

Soldiers

Players: Any number

You will need:
Two chairs

A chair is placed at either end of the room and when the music begins, all of the players must march around them like soldiers in single file. Whenever the music stops, they must perform the task set by their sergeant major. This could be anything from drill with a broom or marching and saluting on the spot to reciting the alphabet backwards. Any player who fails the inspection will be thrown in the guardhouse and will thus miss the remainder of the game. The sergeant major continues with the exercises until just one soldier remains.

Feelers

Players: Any number

You will need:
Music, feather dusters

This saucy derivation of 'Musical Statues' sees players dancing around in a state of undress until the music stops. Then they must 'freeze' and, in the case of someone who is down to her bra and knickers, probably quite literally. Armed with a feather duster, the host or hostess strolls among the scantily-clad statues for 10 seconds and attempts to tickle their fancy before the music starts up again. Anyone moving so much as a muscle drops out and joins in the tickling for the next round, which is actually more fun than doing the dancing. The last player left in wins the game.

Musical Numbers

Players: Any number

You will need:
Music

Watch your guests dance merrily around the room, but then suddenly stop the music and call out a number — 'threes', 'sixes', 'sevens' or whatever. The players immediately have to form groups of that number, anyone who fails to join a group being out. The last player left in emerges as the victor. If you want a short game, call out 'nines' when there are only eight players.

The Blind Conductor

Players: Any number

You will need:
Blindfold, pencil

All of the players stand in a circle except for one person in the middle who is blindfolded and holding a pencil. This is the conductor's baton. The conductor waves his baton merrily while the other players walk round in a circle singing or humming a well-known tune, but when he or she suddenly stops, the players in the circle also must stop immediately. The conductor then points to one of the players who has to sing the song alone, in a disguised voice if necessary. The conductor has to guess who is singing. If the guess is successful, the two players change places; if unsuccessful, the players in the circle all start singing a new song and the conductor has to try again.

Simon Sings

Players: Any number

For this musical version of 'Simon Says', you sing out instructions to your players. It's similar to the well-known 'Simon Says' rules. If the command begins 'Simon sings do this', the players must follow suit, but if the order starts with: 'Do that', they must not copy. Any player who fails to obey an instruction is out. This game should be played at break-neck speed so that everyone becomes thoroughly disorientated.

Musical Sticks

Players: 5-10

You will need:
A garden cane or umbrella, music

The players sit in a circle and one of them is given a garden cane, an umbrella or some form of stick. When the music starts, the player with the stick taps one end on the floor three times and passes it to the player on his or her right. This person repeats the performance and the stick continues its journey until the music stops. Whoever is left holding the stick at that point is eliminated. As players fear the music is about to stop, the tapping will become increasingly frantic. The last player left wins.

I Am The Music Man

Players: 5-10

The first music man sings out: 'I am the music man, I come from down your way and I can play.' At which the others query:, 'What can you play?' Imitating perhaps the actions and noise of a trombone, the music man declares: 'I play the slide trombone.' The next in line assumes the mantle. 'I am the music man, I come from down your way and I can play.' 'What can you play?' Copying the first player's performance, he replies:, 'I play the slide trombone', adding perhaps 'and the piano,' whereupon he does an impression of Elton John or Mrs. Mills. The game continues with each player repeating the sequence and adding a new instrument. Anyone who fails to adhere to the correct order or who can't think of an instrument has to drop out. This game can last as long as a symphony, by which time if you hear that yet another music man comes from down your way, you'd probably want to move house.

Grab

Players: Any uneven number

For this traditional game, all the players except one choose partners and parade around the room singing the following to the tune of your choice:

'There was a jolly miller who lived by himself
As the wheel went round he made his wealth.
One hand in the hopper, the other in the bag
As the wheel went round he made a grab.'

On the word 'grab', everyone must swap partners, including the singleton. After an unseemly scramble for a mate, reminiscent of the Top Rank on a Saturday night when the smoochy songs begin, whoever is left without a partner becomes the poor miller for the next round.

Musical Islands

Players: Any number

You will need:
Pieces of newspaper, music

Tear up some pieces of newspaper and scatter half a dozen or so (depending on the number of players) around the room to represent islands. When the music starts, the players dance around in a circle, but as soon as it stops, they must stand on an island. More than one player may stand on one island. Anyone who fails to find dry ground is considered to have been drowned — heartless, isn't it? After each round, an island is removed so that it becomes more difficult for the players to find sanctuary. The last player left in is the winner.

Next Lines

Players: Any number

Pre-record on to tape, a number of well-known songs. Play them back to your audience but then press the pause button at a crucial moment and ask them to sing out the next line. The first player to sing the right words earns a point. The song should only be paused when most people would be able to identify it. In the case of a particularly distinctive intro, this could be before the first line, but usually it will be at the beginning of the chorus. Points should be deducted for singing like a cat on heat.

The Grand Ball

Players: Any even number of men and women

You will need:
Balloons, music

Guests are randomly given inflated balloons and must then seek out a member of the opposite sex with the same colour balloon. When everyone is paired off, the couples wedge their balloons between their knees and form a circular chain by holding hands. As the music starts, the whole chain shuffles around the room in time to the music, all those who drop or burst their balloon are disqualified along with their partner. The game continues until just one pair are left in the chain.

Pass the Parcel

Players: Any number

You will need:
An object, wrapping paper, music

Wrap a small object in layer upon layer of paper so that it assumes the guise of a sizeable parcel. The players sit in a circle and pass the parcel in a clockwise direction while the music is playing. Whoever is holding the parcel at the moment the music stops is eliminated. The last person left in unwraps the parcel and claims the prize.

Pass the Parcel – the Sequel

Players: Any number

You will need:
An object, wrapping paper, music

In a more caring version of 'Pass the Parcel', whoever is holding the parcel when the music stops is permitted to remove one layer of wrapping. Nobody drops out and the person who removes the last layer of paper keeps the prize. Make sure that the parcel stays on the move while the music is playing to stop avaricious guests trying to hog it and thereby seize the mystery treasure.

Surprise Package

Players: Any number

You will need:
An object, wrapping paper, music

The preparation for this game is the same as for 'Pass the Parcel' except that in each layer of wrapping you should write a forfeit. When the music stops, the player holding the parcel undoes a layer and has to perform the forfeit contained within. If nobody is holding the parcel, the last person who touched it has to suffer the terrible ignominy of the forfeit. Suitable wheezes include:

Hopping around on one leg, shouting 'Pieces of eight, pieces of eight' (not to be given to anyone with an artificial leg)

Singing *Orville's Song* as Orville

Drinking a glass of water with a teaspoon

Reciting *Little Bo Peep* in a thick Birmingham accent (not for parties in the West Midlands)

Waltzing around the room with a lamp stand (don't forget to unplug it first)

Arches

Players: Any even number

You will need:
Music

Two pairs of players line up, one standing at each end of the room, and join hands and raise them above their heads to form an arch. The others players also pair off and, when the music begins, they dance through the arches. When the music stops, the arches lower their arms to ensnare any couples who happened to be passing through at the time. Any pair caught then form another arch, with the game continuing until only one pair remain.

TV Themes

Players: Any number

This is a job for the party's resident couch potato. He or she should hum, whistle or warble a succession of musical themes to well-known TV programmes — things like *Bonanza*, *Only Fools and Horses* and *EastEnders*. The first player to call out the correct answer gains a point.

Circle Line

Players: Any even number

You will need:
Music

This game can also serve as a useful ice-breaker at parties. The players form two circles, an inner and an outer. The women stand in the inner circle and the men in the outer. The two circles should be facing each other. When the music starts, the circles dance round in opposite directions. When it stops, the host calls out a subject and everyone must talk to the person opposite on that topic for a minute. It could be anything from a detailed analysis of the lyrics of *Funky Moped* to the virtues of clean underwear. As the music re-starts, the circles head off in opposite directions once more and a further one-minute conversation ensues, on a different topic. The game ends when everyone is fed up of dancing or talking, or when some couples have hit it off so well that they've disappeared into the bedroom.

Ring Round

Players: Any even number

You will need:
Music

The set-up for this game is the same as for 'Circle Line' with women and men forming two circles, one circle inside the other, and dancing round to the music in opposite directions. But this time when the music stops, the players facing each other must perform a nominated forfeit. So if the host calls out: 'Bray like a donkey', the room will suddenly resemble Blackpool beach. The game continues until most players have performed a forfeit with each other or until everyone has had enough.

Musical Chairs

Players: Any number

You will need:
Chairs, music

At some time in his life Oscar Wilde must have said: 'He who hasn't played Musical Chairs hasn't lived.' And the old favourite makes a splendid adult party game with the addition of a few forfeits. Place the chairs — one fewer than the number of players — in a circle with the seats facing outwards. The players dance around to the music in a carefree manner until the moment the music stops, when they make a dive for the nearest chair. Whoever fails to find a seat has to perform a forfeit and suffers the added pain of elimination. A chair is removed and the band strike up the music once more, the game continuing until there's just one player left.

Lap Top

Players: Any uneven number

You will need:
Chairs, music

Arrange a circle of chairs, one chair for every two players. Sit half of the guests in the chairs and get the other half plus one to dance around to the music. When the music stops, the dancers leap on to the nearest lap, unless it's someone with whom they would rather avoid physical contact, in which case they seek an alternative lap at the risk of being eliminated, because the person who fails to find a lap is out. For the next round, one chair and lap are removed and play continues à la 'Musical Chairs' until there's just one dancer left. It's interesting to observe how some people will sit on absolutely anybody's lap rather than face losing the game.

Anticipation

Players: Any number

You will need:
Music

One person is chosen to operate the music and stands with his or her back to the other players who are seated on the floor or on chairs. They have to anticipate whenever the operator is about to switch off the music, by watching for tell-tale signs. For when the music is turned off, they have to stand up immediately. Anyone rising while the music is still playing is eliminated, as is the last person to get up once the sounds have ceased. The game continues until one player remains.

Musical Spoons

Players: Any number

You will need:
Spoons, music, blindfolds (optional)

This is not a game for those who wish to emerge from the party with their dignity intact. Scatter a number of spoons on the floor, one fewer than there are players. At the sound of music, the players crawl about the floor, endeavouring to maintain as much rhythm as is possible on all-fours. When the music stops, everyone tries to grab a spoon. One unlucky individual is out. Before the music starts again, a spoon is removed and the game carries on until there are two players left fighting over a solitary spoon. The winner of that tussle is the overall victor. To make the game even more interesting, it can be played blindfolded which will probably lead to a lot of groping in the dark. And if it doesn't, play it again until everyone gets the message.

Musical Hats

Players: Any number

You will need:
Hats, music

Seated in a circle, all the players except one are given hats of some shape or form. A good selection of headgear makes for a more entertaining game – such as a sou'wester, a floral bonnet and a crash helmet. When the music starts, the players pass round the hats and when it stops, anyone holding a hat puts it on their head. The player left hatless retires from the proceedings, taking away a hat for good measure. The game continues until only one player remains.

Instrumental

Players: Any number

One player acts as the conductor with the rest as the orchestra. At random, the conductor points to a member of the orchestra and calls out the name of a musical instrument. The chosen person then has to imitate both the sound and the playing action of that instrument. If the rendition is judged hopelessly inaccurate, that player is sacked from the orchestra. The game ends when the full orchestra has been reduced to a soloist. Start with relatively easy instruments — trumpet, flute, violin — before graduating to the likes of cor anglais, flugelhorn and clavichord.

Avoid the Cushion

Players: Any number

You will need:
A cushion, music

A cushion is placed on its end in the centre of the room and the players form a circle around it. When the music starts, the players link arms and dance around the cushion. The aim of every player is to pull someone else over the cushion while at the same time trying to prevent themselves being subjected to the same fate. Anyone who knocks over the cushion is eliminated. The last player dancing round the cushion wins the game but looks a complete idiot.

Musical Hotch Potch

Players: Any number

You will need:
Assorted small objects, music

A pile of small objects, one fewer than the number of players, is placed in the middle of the room. When the music starts, each player dives for an article from the pile and holds it up for the judge to see. The poor unfortunate who did not manage to claim an item is ruled out. Before the next round, one item is removed and the game continues in the traditional manner until only one player is left. Unless you've been desperate to get rid of that china anteater which the mother-in-law bought six Christmases ago, it's advisable to choose unbreakable objects as the 'Musical Hotch Potch' scrum can get quite physical.

Maestro!

Players: Any number

One player assumes the role of conductor and assigns each of the other players a specific musical instrument. When the conductor starts to clap, all the players must play their imaginary instruments, complete with actions and sounds. When the conductor stops clapping and indicates a particular instrument (maybe by drawing a pretend bow across an invisible cello), all the players except the cellist must stop playing immediately. Any musician who continues playing after the conductor has changed to another is eliminated, as is anyone who doesn't spot that the conductor has switched to his or her instrument. The best results will be achieved by a lightning conductor who swaps instruments with great frequency.

NOT IN FRONT OF THE VICAR

Spankety-Spank

Players: 4-8

You will need:
A chair

Even if you don't know S & M from M & S, you'll be hard-pushed to play this game without deriving a modicum of pleasure. One person sits in a chair while another kneels in front with his or her head buried in the other's lap. For the sake of harmony, it is best if the two who at least start in these positions do not harbour a mutual loathing. The rest of the party skip delightfully around this little scenario, pausing en route to spank the bottom of the kneeler. Depending on whose posterior this is, the spank may take the form of a gentle caress or a full-blooded thwack. The kneeler's job is to guess the identity of any of the spankers, although if the kneeler is happy where his face is, he may not be in too much of a hurry to do so. When a spanker is recognised, it's that person's turn to kneel and to choose someone else to sit in the chair. There are no winners, but the kneeler invariably comes up with a smile.

The Blanket Game

Players: 1, plus an eager audience

You will need:
A blanket

Before deciding to play this trick game, choose your victim with care. Make sure it's someone who'll see the funny side — even if it takes a week or two for them to get it. The game begins with the victim seated fully clothed under a large blanket. He (we'll assume for the purposes of this description that a man has been chosen) is told that everyone present has in mind a certain article which he has about his person. He is told that he must guess the article by taking it off and showing it to the entire party. Then and only then will they say

if it was the right article. He is also told that he can't ask any questions to assist him. Unless the man is a complete exhibitionist, he'll more than likely begin by removing his watch, a ring, a sock, his toupée, all of which receive a negative response from the audience. On and on he goes, stripping off down to the bare essentials, and still he can't guess the correct item. Finally when he is totally naked and puzzled, the gleeful onlookers reveal that the article in question is the blanket itself! Of course, the game can be played with two people of the opposite sex under the blanket but there's a danger that you won't get them out afterwards.

Desire

Players: Any even number

You will need:
A pack of playing cards

Discard the picture cards and the aces from an ordinary pack of playing cards so that you're left with the numbers from two to 10. The game is played by pairs with the rest of the ensemble looking on, waiting anxiously for their turn. As host, you can exercise your power by nominating the pairs or you may prefer to allow them to choose for themselves. The first couple sit together and each pick a card without revealing the number. Without speaking (although sighing, moaning and grunting are permitted), they must proceed to act out the strength of their desire for each other, as determined by the numbers on their respective cards. The higher the card, the more intense the desire. At the end of the demonstration, the audience have to try to guess both numbers. If both participants draw a 10, it may be necessary to have a bucket of cold water at hand.

Kiss, Piggy, Kiss

Players: Any number

You will need:
A blindfold

The players form a circle around one person who is blindfolded. They then prance around for a minute holding hands while the blindfolded one turns on the spot in the opposite direction. At the end of the minute, he or she fumbles around for the first available person in the circle and kisses them full on the mouth. From that fleeting moment of passion, he or she must try to recognise the owner of the mouth. In the event of a correct guess, the blindfold's removed and handed over to the kissee who then takes a turn in the middle. But if the blindfolded person fails to recognise the lips, or simply fancies another snog, he or she tries all over again. In the interests of safety, a time limit should be set on each kiss as it has been known for the fire brigade to be called out to prise lips apart.

Contortionists

Players: Any even number of men and women

The players divide up into pairs — one man and one woman. Given the nature of this game, it's probably best if the couple are closely acquainted or, at the very least, not allergic to each other. The object of the exercise is for the pair to change into each other's clothes while still maintaining some form of physical contact — touching feet, holding hands or anything else they can manage. In the name of decency and, in some cases hygiene, all underwear should be kept on. The first couple to swap clothing without infringing the rules win the game.

The Cross-Dressing Derby

Players: 4-8

You will need:
A supply of clothes (men's and women's)

Dig out an assortment of clothes — men's and women's — and place them in separate piles at one end of the room. Each pile should contain a complete outfit — shoes, stockings or socks, underwear, skirt or trousers, shirt or blouse and hat. The competitors line up at the other end of the room — the men opposite the women's clothes and vice versa. On the command 'Go!', each of the players run across to their respective pile and put on the first item of clothing, which could be a problem with burly men trying to squeeze into women's knickers. They then race back to the starting point, touch the wall and dash to put on another item. The first player to arrive back at the starting line, with every item of clothing somewhere about their body, is the winner and gets to change back into his or her own clothes.

Scoop!

Players: 3-8

You will need:
Pencil and paper

The first person thinks of a word to feature in a suitably lurid newspaper headline, the sort of thing you find in the *News of the World*. If the first player suggests 'NUNS', the second player has to think of a word to be added before or after, perhaps 'NAUGHTY'. And so it continues round the room with each player adding a word until the presses roll with something like NAUGHTY NUNS IN SEX ROMP WITH BAWDY BISHOP. It is best to limit the number of words to a maximum of 10, although you can always tag on a subsidiary heading such as — Defrocked in the Vestry'.

Pass the Orange

Players: Any number

You will need:
Oranges

Who would have thought that the humble orange could fulfil such an intimate role at a party? But thanks to this game, countless future partners first set eyes on each other across a juicy Jaffa. The players line up in teams of four or five. Each team is equipped with an orange. The first player places the orange under his or her chin and passes it to the next player's chin. Hands must not be used. The orange continues its journey in this fashion down the line and is then returned in the same way back to the first player. The first team to complete these two lengths is declared the winner. Any team which drops its orange en route must return to the start.

Cheers!

Players: Any number

You will need:
A table bearing a number of small glasses of drink, the lid of a biscuit tin, a carrot

For this drinking game, the players sit around a table laden with drinks and pass a carrot between them while one person taps away on the lid of a biscuit tin or some other item which will create a drumming sound. A full-scale drum kit is a trifle excessive for this game as it may incur the wrath of the Neighbourhood Watch. When the beat on the lid ceases, whoever is holding the carrot knocks back the contents of the glass of their choice. The game continues until all of the glasses are empty. The significance of the carrot remains a mystery.

Scoop Consequences

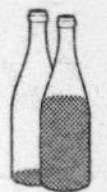

Players: Any number

You will need:
Pencils and paper

'Scoop' can also be played as a form of written consequences with five contributors for each headline. Either multiple or single words can be used. To make the game work, the first word should be an adjective, the second should be a noun, the third should be a verb, the fourth the object of the verb and the fifth a location. The first word is written at the top of the paper which is then handed to the next player. He or she adds another word, folds the paper to conceal the first word, and passes it on. Each time the paper is passed on, only the last-written word should be visible. The end product could be something along the lines of: GUN-TOTING POODLES ROB PET SHOP IN HIGH STREET — Police Looking For Leads.

Feeding the Baby

Players: Any even number

You will need:
Babies' bottles, bibs, drinks

Most men regress to childhood at least once a day, so what better than to take them back to the time when they were babies? 'Feeding the Baby' — and before you get too excited, this is bottle-feeding, not breast-feeding — begins with the women sitting on chairs at one end of the room, holding bibs and babies' bottles half-filled with something like lager or Lucozade, or even champagne for the well-heeled infant. Meanwhile, the men stand at the other end of the room. On the command 'Go!', they rush over to their partners and sit on their laps — for which they'll no doubt need minimum of encouragement — where the women tie bibs around their necks. The men then suck on the teat of the bottle as fast as they can. The men are allowed to grip onto their 'mother' but mustn't touch the bottle with their hands. Once the bottle is empty, the woman unties the bib and she and 'baby' run back to the starting line, the first pair home win. The situation can then be reversed with the men feeding the women.

Cardinal Puff

Players: Any number

You will need:
Plenty of alcohol

A game for dedicated drinkers only, 'Cardinal Puff' (or 'Colonel Bogey' as it is sometimes known) starts with everyone sitting around a table with a full glass in front of them. The first player stands up and proposes a toast 'to the health of Cardinal Puff'. He then embarks on a curious ritual, tapping the top of the table, first with the fore finger of his left hand, then with the forefinger of his right hand, before repeating the process on the underside of the table. He then taps his left leg with the right-hand finger, his right leg with the left-hand finger, his left ear with his left-hand finger and his right ear with the right-hand finger. Finally he picks up the glass with his thumb and one finger, stands, bows once to his fellow drinkers, takes one sip and taps the glass once on the table. No sooner does he sit down than he is up on his feet again, proposing another toast 'to the health of Cardinal Puff Puff'. He repeats the entire process, but this time using two fingers and tapping twice at each stage. He rounds it off by bowing twice to his fellow revellers, taking two sips from the glass and tapping it twice on the table. He then rises to his feet for a third time and announces a drink 'to the health of Cardinal Puff Puff Puff' before going through the routine with three fingers and in triplicate. Throughout these three toasts, his drinking companions will be watching eagle-eyed for the slightest deviation from the rules, knowing only too well that any error means he has to start all over again. Of course, it has been known for some players to make a mistake deliberately, simply so that they can have another drink. When you wake up the following morning (or maybe even the day after that), the one guarantee is that you'll wish you had stuck to something like 'Musical Chairs' instead.

Scrimmage

Players: 10 or more

You will need:
A length of tape or string

If you've ever wondered what it would be like to host a full-blooded rugby scrum in your front room, here's your chance to find out. Two teams of roughly equal strength (not necessarily equal numbers) line up, heads down, in scrum style across a line of tape or string drawn down the centre of the room. By pushing, shoving and thrusting, each team tries to force itself over the line and prevent the other team from doing so. The team which gets every member across the line is the winner. The amount of dress worn for this game is optional, but bear in mind that the average scrum contains much mauling, tugging and groping of buttocks.

Strip Taboo

Players: 4-8

The rules here are the same as for ordinary 'Taboo' except that whoever is guilty of uttering the forbidden letter has to remove an item of clothing as punishment. Extroverts may choose to wear practically nothing and then deliberately try to say the banned letter. Those who are more reserved, however, may either skip this pastime altogether or dress up in layer upon layer of clothing so that by the time there is any danger of an inch or two of bare flesh being revealed, everyone will have lost interest.

Malicious Rumours

Players: Any number

You will need:
Pencil and paper

While one of your guests leaves the room, the other players huddle together and each tries to think up an item of gossip about the person outside. These rumours may contain an element of truth or they can be totally fictional, depending upon the sensitivities of the people involved. They could be anything from 'He only changes his socks once a week' to 'She even irons the face flannels'. Each item of gossip is written down next to the name of the rumour-monger and when the victim returns, the list of accusations is read out. The victim must attempt to match each rumour with the person responsible for spreading it, two points being awarded for a correct pairing. When the whole list has been discussed, the points are added up and the next player leaves the room while the first player finds out who really did say she slept with the milkman — and his horse. When everyone has had a turn, the player with the highest points total is declared the winner.

Key Chain

Players: 3 or more

You will need:
A key, a length of string

The number of people able to play this game at any one time is governed by the answer to a simple question: How long is a piece of string? For the longer the string, the more players it can accommodate. The game is played with a key on a length of string. The players stand in a line — men and women alternating — and have to thread themselves onto the string. The first player threads the key down the inside of his clothes from the top of his shirt to the bottom of his trousers. The woman next to him then threads it up the inside of her clothes from her skirt to her neck, and so it continues along the line. There are no winners or losers but it can be a titillating experience, particularly if the dastardly host has placed the key in the freezer before the game...

Sounds Sexy

Players: Any number

The challenge here is to think of as many sexy words as possible, each beginning with the last letter of the previous player's word. The players sit in a circle and play proceeds in a clockwise direction. Any player unable to think of a word, or whose word is not deemed sufficiently sexy by the rest of the party, has to perform a suitable forfeit decided upon by the others. The degree of embarrassment of this game depends upon the nature of its forfeits. Players may defend the sexiness of their word vigorously in a bid to escape the forfeit. For example, if the 'Sounds Sexy' word sequence goes, 'sensual, lust, Thompson', the last player may argue that he finds Emma Thompson incredibly sexy. It is for the rest of the group to decide whether such feelings are likely.

Tricky Predicaments

Players: Any number

You will need:
Pencils and paper

In advance of the party, you need to think up a number of bizarre predicaments, one per player. Each situation will form the climax of a story, hastily composed by the guest to whom it has been assigned. Deal out your endings to the most appropriate players and then allow each three minutes to produce a story which might plausibly lead up to the finale. Then get them to read out their efforts, a prize going to the most imaginative composition. Here are a few predicaments to give you an idea of what is required:

'The last thing I had expected was to have sex with a guardsman, especially in the middle of Trooping the Colour.'

'And that's how I came to be chained to a topless model on my stag night.'

'I never realised I could derive so much pleasure from a banana until I met Peter.'

'And the next thing I knew I was sucking strawberry ice cream off the toes of a High Court judge.'

'The plumber looked at me, ballcock in hand, and I instinctively knew that the ironing would have to wait.'

A Tender Behind

Players: 6 or more

This is very much a game of surprise. One man starts chugging round the room like a train and invites a woman who takes his fancy to be his tender behind. She places her arms around his hips and they chug out of the room. When they are out of sight and earshot, he goes to kiss her but at the last moment gives her a playful slap instead. She is naturally aggrieved until he explains to her that it's all part of the game. So they rejoin the throng and pick another man to join the train. Once out of the room, the first man kisses the woman and she goes to kiss the second man, but slaps him gently instead. When a fourth person joins in, player one kisses player two, player two kisses player three, and player three feigns to kiss player four before changing it to a slap. With growing anticipation, further carriages are recruited, only to be rewarded initially with a slap in the face before the kissing begins. The game continues until everyone has joined the train, but spare a thought for the poor soul who is last to be picked and therefore misses out on all the kissing and just receives the slap in the face. To avoid occupying that unwanted position, go easy on the garlic dip.

Loud and Low

Players: Any number

You will need:
A saucepan, a wooden spoon

This is a variation of the children's game 'Hot and Cold' where you used to say, 'getting warmer, very warm, hot, boiling hot' until the searcher found the hidden object. Here, the indication of proximity is made not in degrees Fahrenheit but by beating on a saucepan with a wooden spoon. The louder the tapping, the closer the hunter is to his or her goal, the final moments being greeted by a veritable wall of sound of which any steel band would be proud.

The game begins with one player being sent from the room and everyone else thinking of something they would really like to see him or her do. Of course, the more risqué the suggestion, the more intruiging the consequences. If the best you can come up with is 'get him to make a nice cup of tea', then you'll probably find your guests leaving before the pubs have shut. Instead, get a man to kiss the woman you know he's fancied for ages or to nibble the earlobes of the local traffic warden. Then when the person returns, the pan-tapper sets to work, skillfully steering him or her towards the chosen target to the feverish anticipation of the onlookers. For this is one of those games where just as much pleasure can be derived from watching as from playing.

Boat Race

Players: 10 or more

In this classic drinking game, players sit on the floor in teams of five or six as if they were members of a rowing crew. Each member of the team has a pint of beer in his hand and a towel wrapped over his shoulders to mop up any spillage. On the command 'Go!', the first player in each team downs the pint as quickly as possible and turns the empty glass upside down on his head. With the glass in place, the second player than guzzles his pint and inverts the glass on his head. Only when that has been done can the third player start drinking. The winning team is the first to have all its members with upturned glasses on their heads.

Naughty Numbers

Players: Any number

Give each player a secret number — the men should have odd numbers, the women even numbers. Arrange your guests in a circle except for one man who is chosen to go in the middle. He then calls out two even numbers whereupon the women with those numbers rush forward to kiss him. The first to do so takes his place in the middle and then calls out two odd numbers, inviting the two men assigned those numbers to come forward for a peck on the cheek or something stronger depending on the level of attraction. Unless you are of a gay disposition, it's advisable to remember which sex has which numbers.

Food-Tasting Relay

Players: 10 or more

You will need:

A quantity of whipped cream, spoons, chairs

Divide the players into teams of five and seat four members of each team in chairs. The fifth member is supplied with a tub of whipped cream (real or synthetic) and has to move along the line spooning a small portion of cream onto the bare flesh of each player. The key rule is that in each case it must be a different part of the anatomy — say a hand, a knee, a cheek or a bald head. Having done the smearing, the player races back to the start and goes down the line, licking off the cream from his or her four team-mates. When the run is completed, that player sits down in the first chair and the previous occupant is handed the tub of cream for a repeat performance. The first team in which all five members have smeared and licked one another is declared the winner. As the competitors race against the clock and the licking becomes more frantic, cream does tend to fly everywhere, so it's worth protecting your floors with plastic sheets.

Whose Feet?

Players: Any number

You will need:
A screen or sheet, pencils and paper

If you haven't washed your feet for a week or boast a distinctive set of verrucas, you'd best give this game a miss. For it requires two teams to try to identify each other from their bare feet. While the first team leave the room, the others remove shoes, socks, tights, corn plasters etc, and position themselves behind a large screen or sheet so that only their ankles and feet are visible. The first team then return for close inspection. They may caress the feet but must not tickle in case the resultant giggle proves identifiable. The inspectors write down their answers and the player with most correct identifications wins the game. The two teams then reverse roles. This is generally a good-natured game although a bit of ill-feeling can creep in if Cindy Rogers, the model, finds her feet mistaken for those of Bert Blatherwick, the builder.

The Catwalk Game

Players: Any number

You will need:
Two volunteer models, clothing, pencils and paper

All of the guests are seated. They are then told that a female model will walk around the room, displaying the latest designer labels, and that they should make a mental note of what she is wearing. When she leaves, the players are handed pencils and paper and told to write down as much as they can remember about her outfit. Obviously the more accessories she can muster — gloves, jewellery, Zimmerframe etc — the better. Next the guests are informed that a male model will be parading on the catwalk and, sure enough, a man enters dressed only in boxer shorts or swimming trunks, whichever is readily accessible. The players are then told that they have two minutes to write down not what he is wearing, but what he will be wearing when he reappears fully dressed. On his return, the lists are checked and a point awarded for every correct prediction. The player with the highest combined total for both models wins the game.

Wagging Tongues

Players: 8 or more

You will need:
Peanuts

This game is best played by people who know each other fairly well, although if they don't at the start, there's a fair chance that they will by the end. The players are divided into teams of four who stand in lines. The aim of the game is to transport a peanut down the line, solely by the use of the players' tongues. No hands are allowed. In the event of swallowing or dropping one's nut, a substitute nut may be introduced but play must go back to the start. Any couple suspected of taking an undue length of time over transferring the nut from one tongue to the next may be hosed down with cold water. The first team to tongue-lift the peanut from one end of the line to the other wins the game.

Buttocks

Players: 3-8

You will need:
Coins, a dish

Apparently a game much loved by royalty down the years, Buttocks certainly lives up to its name. It invites players to transport a coin between their clenched buttocks from one end of the room to the other and to deposit it in a dish. Hands may only be used for the initial loading process. The player who has deposited most coins at the end of five minutes wins the game. For fear of accidents, it's best if this activity is played fully clothed, but even then 5p pieces should be avoided because of their size and the hard edges of 50p coins can chafe... er, apparently.

Fantasies

Players: Any number

You will need:
Pencils and cards

Players are asked to write down their secret fantasies, restricting their ideas to present company and surroundings. Their cards are collected, shuffled and re-distributed among the gathering. Where feasible, they must then undertake the prescribed task. Should the suggestion be too outrageous, they can refuse on the grounds that it may incriminate them. If they're really lucky, they'll be able to act out their own fantasy — although of course it will now become public knowledge — or conversely they may find themselves obliged to writhe around on the floor with Mrs. Blenkinsop. Should the card fall to Mr. Blenkinsop, he may choose to pass. When all of the suitable ideas have been performed, everyone must try to guess which fantasy belonged to whom. This is probably the most embarrassing part of the whole game.

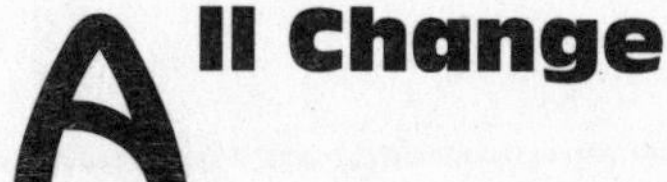

All Change

Players: Equal numbers of men and women

With the players pairing off into male/female couples, switch off the lights for two minutes. There then follows much groping in the dark and fumbling with bra straps as the couples attempt to swap as many clothes as possible. The pair who have put on the most of each other's clothes when the lights are turned back on are the winners.

Dream Date

Players: 5-10

You will need:
Pencils and paper

Choose two players (one man, one woman) who are to select partners for their blind date. Get each of them to write down a list of three questions which they would put to a potential suitor — such as 'Where would you take me on a dream date?'; 'Which celebrity do you think you most resemble, and why?'; 'Do you believe in sex before Match of the Day?' Then get each of the women to write down their answers to the man's questions and each of the men to compose their replies to the woman's. Beginning with the woman, and taking each question at a time, read out the men's answers without disclosing who wrote them. After listening to the replies, the woman must decide who she would choose to accompany her on their date. Only then is the author of the answers revealed. This can be a harrowing moment... The process is then repeated with the man listening to the women's responses.

Postman's Knock

Players: Any number

No party is complete without this all-time favourite. One male guest is chosen to be the postman and as such has to leave the room. Meanwhile, the rest of the players are given numbers — even for the men, odd for the women. When they're ready, the postman knocks on the door and announces that he has something for a certain house number (odd) and adds 'Come and get it!' The woman with that number duly obliges and goes out to join the postman who tries to prove himself to be a first-class male by giving her a kiss. The pair return to the room and one of the women takes over the sorting bag in the guise of postmistress. The other players choose new numbers and the postmistress knocks to announce that she has something for a house with an even number. The occupant goes out to receive his kiss and the game continues until everyone in the street has a smile on their face.

Choices

Players: Any number

You will need:
Pencils and paper

The players sit in a circle and all compile lists of four people of the opposite sex. Each person's list is then passed on to the person immediately on their right. Faced with someone else's selection — the names can be celebrities or fellow party guests — the players have to explain their significance. For example, if a woman receives a list reading, 'Tom Cruise, John Cleese, Murray Walker and Mr. Watts, the local greengrocer', she may reveal that Tom Cruise is the person she'd most like to have an affair with, John Cleese is the person most likely to make her laugh, Murray Walker is the person she would least like to employ as a librarian, and the local greengrocer is the person she is most likely to get her oats from. The most imaginative set of answers wins a prize.

The Feather Game

Players: 3-8

You will need:
A blanket, a feather

A large blanket is draped across the floor and all of the players sit beneath it, fully-clothed, pulling it up to their chin. Someone throws a feather into the air and everybody starts puffing furiously... and with good reason. For the penalty for allowing the feather to be blown over your shoulder is to remove an item of clothing which must then be raised above the blanket as proof. If one person is soon obliged to hoist a number of trophies aloft, there will be a discernible shift beneath the blanket as other players try to move closer to him or her. This is therefore one game where the loser can most definitely end up the winner.

Banana Twist

Players: Even numbers of men and women

You will need:
A supply of bananas

The players split up into male/female pairs and each pair are given a banana. The man stands with his legs apart, rather like the Sheriff of Nottingham's men used to do in *The Adventures of Robin Hood*, and, on the command 'Go!', the woman has to use her hands to cajole the banana up the inside of the right leg of his trousers and down the left leg, the first banana to emerge from the bottom of the left leg earning victory. The push and squeeze is the favoured method and obviously the descent is much easier unless he happens to be wearing drainpipes. Inevitably, the tricky bit is across the top. Either route can be taken — fore or aft — but at no time may the man lend a hand. Nor may trousers be removed to free a trapped banana. If a banana does become lodged, you simply have to try to grin and bear it.

IN FULL SWING

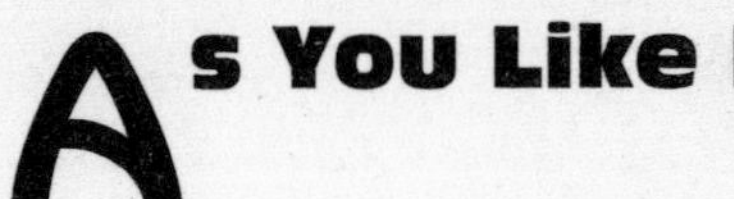

As You Like It

Players: Any number

You will need:
Pencils, name cards for each guest

Cards are prepared, each bearing the name of one of the guests, and are divided into two piles according to sex. Each woman is asked to draw a man's card and vice-versa. All of the guests are told to write some action or stunt — the more outrageous the better — on the card. It could be anything from singing *Like a Virgin* in just bra and knickers to downing a pint in one go or passionately kissing the hostess. Then comes the catch. Everyone assumes that the person named on the card has to perform the dubious deed but instead the host asks each player to read out what they have written and says: 'If that's what you want, let's see you do it!' Cue gross embarrassment...

Spanish Inquisition

Players: Any number

The players sit in a circle except for one person standing in the middle who acts as inquisitor and thinks up three categories — perhaps fish, American states and movie stars. Displaying the aggressive tactics which made Torquemada's reputation, the inquisitor points at a particular player, shouts out a category and demands an instant answer, such as 'halibut' if the category is fish. A split second later, he will be pointing at another unfortunate and yelling out a different category or maybe the same one. Again the reply must be immediate. Alternatively, he may even wish to persecute the same player on up to three successive occasions (the maximum allowed). The punishment for failing to give an answer straight away, or repeating an earlier answer, is elimination from the game... unless of course there happens to be a rack handy.

The Grapefruit Shuffle

Players: 8 or more

You will need:
Two grapefruits

Two teams of equal numbers sit on the floor facing each other with their legs outstretched. The game then begins with the host placing a grapefruit on the ankles of the first player in each team and they then have to pass the fruit down the line as quickly as possible without using any other part of their anatomy. Should the grapefruit fall off or roll away, the offending team then has to start all over again. The winning team is the first one to finish the whole course. For those who like to throw all convention to the wind, this game can also be played with an orange.

Superlatives

Players: Any number

You will need:
Brown paper, string, sticky label, a small prize

This variation on 'Pass the Parcel' requires you to prepare a number of layers of brown paper, each layer tied with string and with a small prize (probably something useless like a broken zip) in the middle. Stuck to each layer is a written label and it is this which indicates to whom the parcel should next be passed. The labels will have written on them things like: 'To the woman with the most beautiful hair', 'To the man with the kindest eyes' or 'To the woman with the longest legs'. If you know all of your guests really well, you could alternatively try descriptions such as: 'To the man with the worst acne', 'To the woman with the biggest feet' or 'To the woman with the smallest boobs'. The rest can be left to your imagination. Suffice to say that the players are seated in a circle and the parcel is handed to one player at random. He or she reads the label on the

outside before handing it to whoever the description seems most applicable. The chosen one then unwraps the second layer and so the game continues until the prize is reached, by which time half of the party will be blushing and the rest will be livid.

Murder in the Dark

Players: 6 or more

You will need:
Slips of paper, a hat

A number of slips of paper are dropped into a hat, one slip per player. All of the pieces of paper are blank except for one which bears a cross and another which bears a circle. The players then pull out the slips. Whoever draws the cross is the Murderer; whoever draws the circle is the Detective. The former remains silent but the latter announces the fact that he or she is now following in the footsteps of Morse or Miss Marple. All of the lights in the house are then switched off and the players move about stealthily. The Murderer locates a likely victim and whispers in their ear 'You're dead' at which the victim falls to the floor and screams loudly. As the Murderer hurries away from the scene, the Detective, hearing the screams, switches on the lights. From the moment the lights are switched on, nobody except the Detective is allowed to move. The Detective proceeds to question the various suspects, all of whom must answer truthfully except for the Murderer who can tell bare-faced lies unless asked directly, 'Are you the Murderer?' when he or she must confess. Naturally the corpse says nothing. If there are fewer than 10 players, the Detective is permitted only two guesses at unmasking the Murderer; if there are more than 10, the Detective has three guesses. This is not a game for those who are afraid of the dark or who have recently served a life sentence.

Grandma's Footsteps

Players: Any number

By the time the party is in full swing and everyone has forgotten any inhibitions they may have had when they arrived, there is more and more scope for including the sort of silly games which are usually played at parties for five and six-year-olds. You will often find that your guests will have more fun playing something like 'Grandma's Footsteps' than an exceedingly clever word game. And if their minds have become addled by alcohol, there is the added bonus of no complicated rules to remember. One person is chosen to be leader and, slowly but purposefully, walks from one end of the room to the other with the remaining players following dutifully behind in crocodile fashion. Suddenly, without warning, the leader will look round. This is the signal for everyone to stop dead in their tracks since anybody whom the leader catches moving is eliminated from the game. This ritual continues, with the leader's turns becoming increasingly frequent, until there is just one player left in the line.

The Last Straw

Players: 8 or more

You will need:
Straws, two thimbles

The players are divided into two teams and are seated in rows facing each other. Each player places a straw in their mouth and a thimble is passed from one end of the team to the other by balancing it delicately on the end of the straws. No hands are allowed and if the thimble is dropped, it can only be picked up by using the straw. When the thimble has been successfully passed along the line, the last player races to the other end and everyone moves up a chair. The game continues as before until all of one team's members are back in their starting positions. With four team members, this will require four

successful runs. Guests with a heavy cold or a nervous twitch are advised to sit this one out.

Water Lot of Fun

Players: 5-10

You will need:
Pen, paper, egg cup, jug of water, towel

You may want to play this sitting on a tropical beach — or, if there isn't one handy, an easily mopped surface will suffice. Granny's best Wilton carpet may not be ideal. Everyone sits in a circle with the props placed inside. One person is chosen at random and sits inside the circle. The chosen person then thinks of a list of items that roughly coincides with the number of people playing the game (not including themselves). So if there are five people, good lists would be all the members of The Beatles, English Sunday newspapers, numbers one to five, days of the week etc. The person in the centre then chooses one item from their list and secretly notes it down. Going round in a clockwise direction, those in the circle name items from the list, never repeating an item. The person who names the item that the water carrier has noted down has the egg cup of water thrown in their face.

Mouth to Mouth Spoons

Players: 8 or more

You will need:
Spoons, two table tennis balls

The players are divided into two equal teams and each issued with a spoon. Standing in lines, they grip the spoons in their mouths by the handles and try to pass a table tennis ball down the line without using their hands. If at any stage of its journey the ball falls to the floor, the guilty team has to begin again. The winning team is the first to pass the ball from one end of the line to the other. To prolong the competition, it can be staged over the best of five games.

Spot the Squeeze

Players: Any number

Players stand in a circle with their hands by their sides while one player stands in the middle. The game starts with one of the circle squeezing the hand of the adjoining player who in turn squeezes the hand of the next person and so on. The player in the centre is trying to spot the squeeze and anyone caught in the act of squeezing has to take his or her place in the middle. To confuse the would-be spotter, the squeeze can suddenly change direction. The nature of the game means that few people are keen to stand next to the local sewage engineer.

Expostulate

Players: Any number

In this entertaining guessing game, one person goes out of the room while the others choose a verb such as 'mash', 'mince', 'kiss' or, if the party has degenerated to that level, 'fornicate'. The person outside returns and tries to guess the verb by asking a question of each player in turn, but in each question, the word 'expostulate' must be used instead of the word being guessed. So a question might be: 'Do I expostulate below the waist?' If the mystery word is 'gargle', the answer would almost certainly be 'No'. Players must only answer 'Yes' or 'No'. The game continues either until the word has been guessed or until the person doing the guessing surrenders. In the latter event, he or she has to pay a sizeable forfeit.

Never, Never, Never

Players: Any number

This one may take some explaining — so don't leave it until everyone has drunk too much. Going round the room, the players take it in turns to announce something that they've *never* done. It doesn't have to be true, the main criterion is that it is something which everyone else present is most likely to have done. So if you declare, 'I've never eaten a sherbert lemon,' you are on fairly safe ground as, there are bound to be plenty of people who've tasted sherbert lemons. However, if you say, 'I've never ridden the winner of the Grand National', whilst it may be perfectly true, it's also unlikely anyone else in the room will have either. Should any of the other players have *not* done what you said you haven't done, you lose one of your three lives. It's complicated — but can be very revealing.

My Aunt Went to Town

Players: Any number

This is another 'round game' where all of the players are seated in a circle. The first player chooses a letter (say, P) and reveals, 'My aunt went to town and bought a piano.' The next player takes up the theme. 'My aunt went to town and bought a piano and a pair of platform shoes.' Player three might continue, 'My aunt went to town and bought a piano, a pair of platform shoes and a platypus.' And on it goes with each succeeding player reciting the previous purchases in correct order and adding another. Anyone who slips up is knocked out of the game, the last person left in is the winner.

Simon Says

Players: Any number

For this hardy perennial, one player assumes the role of Simon and issues orders to the remainder of the throng. If the leader declares: 'Simon says pat your bottom', then everyone must pat their bottom. But if he or she simply orders, 'Pat your bottom', they must not copy the action, anyone who does so being eliminated. Only instructions prefixed by the words 'Simon says' must be obeyed. The game is best played fast and furious with the last person left in emerging as the winner.

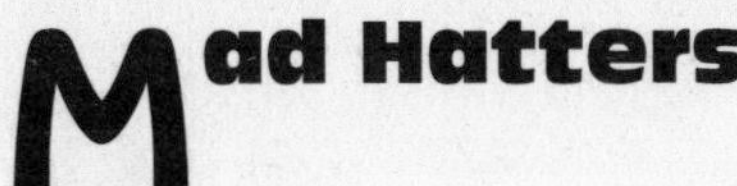

Mad Hatters

Players: 2 plus an audience

You will need:
Two hats

A player enters the room carrying two hats. He or she puts one hat on his or her own head and hands the other hat to a second player. From then on, the second player must ensure that all his or her actions and words are as opposite as possible to those of the first player. So, if player one scratches the top of his or her head, player two should follow by scratching the sole of a foot. The rest of the party sit in judgement and anyone who is deemed to have slipped up makes way for another player. The winner is the one who can maintain the performance for the longest.

Farmyard Frolic

Players: 8 or more

You will need:
An assortment of sweets

The players split up into teams of four, one of whom is the leader. The team members have to adopt the identity of a different animal, complete with actions and noises, but no smells please. Even so, anyone masquerading as a skunk should be given a wide berth. This is all easy enough for those who collar dog, cat, cow or horse, but the likes of marmoset, gerbil, armadillo or iguana require greater imagination. Leaving the team leaders in the lounge, the animals set off in search of the sweets which have been scattered around the house by the host. When a player finds a sweet, he or she makes a noise like the chosen animal to alert the team leader who goes to collect it. It is therefore important that the leaders remember which animals are in their team. After 15 minutes, the team whose leader has collected the most sweets wins the game.

Shopping List

Players: Any even number

You will need:
Slips of paper, pencils

In this game, two teams go on an imaginary shopping trip without the hazards of having to steer a supermarket trolley with a mind of its own. On separate slips of paper, write 20 anagrams of items you could purchase at a typical supermarket and arrange the slips on a table. The two team leaders send one member of their shopping expedition at a time to the table to fetch an item. The happy shopper picks up a slip, takes it to the leader and — after it has been decoded — returns it to the table. Then it is the turn of the next team member. When the leader has deciphered all 20 items, the list goes through the checkout and if it is correct, victory is claimed. If you are not used to the rigours of the supermarket, here are 20 anagrams to save you some time:

Shif Grinsef (Fish Fingers)
Kenhicc (Chicken)
Shuntudog (Doughnuts)
Rulof (Flour)
Membercat (Camembert)
Sumose (Mousse)
Scissortan (Croissants)
Poshmoa (Shampoo)
Act Tritle (Cat Litter)
Slabi (Basil)
Rwiserbreast (Strawberries)
Ilteto Lorls (Toilet Rolls)
Spircs (Crisps)
Suetsis (Tissues)
Catpek Upso (Packet Soup)
Moledean (Lemonade)
Seasgasu (Sausages)
Stibsuci (Biscuits)
Nooni Grins (Onion Rings)
Stoatpetho (Toothpaste)

Pass the Bottle

Players: 10 or more

You will need:
Two empty bottles

The players line up in two teams with an empty bottle standing on the floor at one end of each line. The first player picks up the bottle between his or her knees and then passes it to the knees of the next person in line. The bottle makes its way along the line in this fashion, the first team to get it to the other end being declared the winner. No hands are allowed and if the bottle is dropped at any stage, it must be picked up with the knees. Women in short, tight skirts may find this game a struggle but their efforts to bend will provide considerable pleasure for others.

Nudge Nudge

Players: Any number

The players are seated on the floor, close together, in a circle. One person is appointed leader. That person sets the ball rolling by nudging the player on his or her left. The nudge is passed around the circle until it arrives back at the leader who then starts a new discipline — perhaps the tweak of an earlobe. This action too is passed around the circle in clockwise fashion and when it reaches the leader once more, a fresh activity is initiated — maybe a peck on the cheek. The game can be played ad infinitum, the only rule being that the participants must keep a straight face at all times. Any sniggering or giggling will result in the guilty party being awarded a forfeit.

Add One

Players: Any number

The players sit in a circle and the first person performs a simple action, such as stamping a foot, clapping hands or sticking out their tongue. The person on his or her left repeats the action but then adds another, maybe raising an eyebrow. The next person on the left repeats the first two moves and adds something else, perhaps the scratching of an armpit. The game continues around the circle in this manner with each player repeating the previous moves in the correct order before adding an invention of his or her own. Anyone unable to remember the sequence has to drop out. The last player left in is the winner.

Beads in the Jar

Players: 3-6

You will need:
Jam jars, beads, knitting needles

For each player, provide one jam jar filled with tiny beads (or any similar-sized round objects) and two knitting needles. Using the knitting needles in one hand like chopsticks, the competitors have to lift as many beads as possible from their jar in three minutes, the highest total being the winner. This game calls for a steady hand and is therefore more entertaining, if less productive, when the guests have had a drink or two.

Good Morning, Madam

Players: Any number

You will need:
A pack of playing cards

This is a grown-ups' version of 'Snap', but here the excitement occurs when a particular card is turned up, rather than two of the same. Using a conventional pack of playing cards, each player in turn plays a card face up. In the event of the card being an ace, a king, a queen or a jack, all of the cards below are captured. But there's more. When an ace is laid, everyone slams down their hand on top of it. When it's a king, everyone stands to attention and salutes. When there's a jack, the players must get to their feet and curtsy. And when a queen is laid, they all shout out at the top of their voices: 'Good morning, Madam.' In each case, the first player to perform the prescribed action gains the booty. The game is over when one player has won all of the cards.

Colonel Blood

Players: Any number

You will need:
A chair, a blindfold, a book

Historians will know Colonel Blood as the man who attempted to steal the Crown Jewels. Here is a chance to follow in his footsteps pursuing a rather more modest booty, a book, from under the nose of a supremely vigilant guard. At least, the guard would be vigilant were it not for the fact that he or she is blindfolded. The person chosen to be guard sits blindfolded on a chair in the middle of the room with the book on the floor next to the chair. The other players hover around and take it in turns to creep up to the book and try to steal it without being detected. If the guard hears a sound, he or she points in the direction from which it came. If that corresponds with the position of one

of the would-be thieves, that particular mission is abandoned and the thief becomes the guard for the next round. This may seem harsh but is a more humane alternative to beheading, which was the usual punishment for jewel thieves. However, the guard must not accuse at random for fear of having to pay a forfeit. Should one of the players succeed in stealing the book undetected, the guard remains in the chair for the next round.

Killer

Players: Any number

You will need:
A pack of playing cards

This fiendish game can spread terror among the most happy-go-lucky of party guests as everyone becomes terrified that they'll be the next to fall victim to the callous killer in their midst. Deal out part of a pack of playing cards — one card for each player — first making sure that the joker is among them. Whoever is dealt the joker becomes the killer but, for obvious reasons, keeps that fact a secret. The killer does his dirty work by winking at his victims, in the process ensuring that nobody else spots the dastardly deed. He does not rest until he has winked at every member of the company, thereby wiping out the whole lot. After being winked at, each victim must wait at least 30 seconds before dying, perhaps by slumping in an armchair or falling theatrically to the floor. Meanwhile,the other players, realising that a killer is on the loose, do their utmost to catch him in the very act of winking. Anyone who believes they have seen the killer at work must challenge the victim before he or she dies, rather than the killer. If the suspicion is confirmed, the killer is apprehended. However, if the accusation proves to be false, it results in the instant death of the accuser — another one for the killer to cross off his list. The silent but deadly goings-on are at their most effective when executed during a seemingly innocuous activity, such as clearing the table or passing round the salted peanuts. For that is the beauty of this game — nobody ever knows when the killer is about to strike. Don't have nightmares.

What is My Thought Like?

Players: 5-10

If you are a medium, or even an extra-large, this mind-reading game will be right up your street. One person is chosen to think of an object (animate or inanimate) and then asks each of the other players in turn: 'What is my thought like?' Mere mortals will presumably have no idea and will resort to making wild guesses. When everyone has made a suggestion, the first person names his or her object and then asks each player to say why their particular object was like the mystery item. Players should be given a few minutes to come up with their answers, a prize being awarded to the most imaginative. Let us assume that the chosen object was Concorde and that various players suggested a tube of glue, the Prime Minister, a tennis racket, a stripogram and a broken zip. The questioning could go:

First player: 'Why is Concorde like a tube of glue?'

Answer: 'Because you can get high on both.'

First player: 'Why is Concorde like the Prime Minister?'

Answer: 'Because both spend most of their time with their head in the clouds.'

First player: 'Why is Concorde like a tennis racket?'

Answer: 'Because both provide first-class service.'

First player: 'Why is Concorde like a stripogram?'

Answer: 'Because both take off twice a day.'

First player: 'Why is Concorde like a broken zip?'

Answer: 'Because one flies through the air and the other lets air through the flies.'

Dead Ants

Players: Any number

Everybody stands around aimlessly, chatting about the price of washing-up liquid or the FT Index, until someone shouts: 'Dead Ants!' At the outbreak of mass insecticide, all of the players lie on the ground with their arms and legs in the air and must attempt to remain absolutely motionless. Any player who makes a movement is disqualified. All of the disqualified ants try to make the others move without physically touching them. Eventually just one dead ant remains and he or she, to mix insect metaphors, becomes the queen bee.

Find Your Mate

Players: Any even number

Another disaster on Noah's Ark! All the animals have escaped on a stormy night and are desperately trying to find their mates. Players participate as pairs of a particular creature — two turkeys, two tigers, two hyenas and so on — and, in total darkness, seek out their partners by calling to each other in the manner of their allotted animal, in other words gobbling, roaring or laughing. The last couple to pair off must pay a forfeit.

Noah's Ark

Players: 7 or more

You will need:
Pencils and paper

Oh calamity! Since the privatisation of Noah's Ark, Group 4 have been introduced to provide security, as a result of which all of the animals have escaped. In order to claim on the insurance, poor old Noah has got to make a list of the missing creatures. Each player takes on two roles — that of one of the animals and of Noah himself. The game begins with you assigning each player the name of a creature which makes a distinctive sound — pig, lion, lamb, frog, wolf, crow, seagull, duck, bee, donkey, goose, cow, horse, cockerel, snake, dog, cat, sea lion etc. Then all of the lights are turned out and everybody starts grunting, roaring, bleating, croaking, howling, cawing, squawking, quacking, buzzing, braying, honking, mooing, neighing, clucking, hissing, barking, miaowing and whatever noise sea lions make, all at the same time. While making the noise of their own animal, the players must also make mental notes of the other sounds they hear because, after five minutes of this mayhem, the lights are switched back on and, now wearing their Noah hats, they must write down the names of as many animals as they can remember hearing. Since you will have kept a check-list of the animals, you can mark the lists and work out who has got the highest total. He or she is the winner.

Mummies

Players: Any even number

You will need:
Rolls of toilet paper

In Oedipus's favourite game, players pair off into couples, ideally one man and one woman. The woman is given a toilet roll and has three minutes in which to wrap her partner from head to foot in toilet paper so that he bares an uncanny resemblance to an Egyptian mummy. The winners are the couple adjudged to have created the most effective mummy.

Ping-Pong Roll

Players: Any number

You will need:
Table tennis balls, lengths of string

The players are divided into pairs and each pair is supplied with a table tennis ball and two pieces of string of equal length (about four feet). The team-mates stand at either end of the string and, with a piece in each hand, hold the lengths taut and fairly close together like railway lines. At the 'off', a non-competitor places the ball at one end of the lines and the player at the other end lowers his or her strings so that the ball can go downhill. When it reaches the far end, the players swap stances so that the ball will now slope back towards the start. Care should be taken not to go too fast as the ball can easily roll off a player's hands at the turning point. Any ball that falls to the floor must be returned to the start of that length. The first team to complete six lengths are the winners.

Family Snap

Players: 6-12

This is a game for the quick-witted. Prior to the party, prepare a list of imaginary names which are sufficiently alike to cause widespread confusion. Each player is given one of these names. For example, if there are 10 players, you could choose:

Mr. James Lindsay
Mr. Lindsay James
Ms. Lindsey James
Sir Lindsley Jameson
Gemma Lindsay
Lynn James
Linda James
Lynn Jameson
Linda Jameson
Jem Lindsay

Inform the players of their names verbally, repeating the list so that it sinks in. Then explain that you are going out to call out a succession of quick-fire names — the ones you have allotted to the players, plus a number of 'ringers' such as James Lynn, Jeremy Lindsay, Gemma James and Jeremy Lynn. When a name is called out and its owner shouts out 'Snap', he or she scores three points. If it's one of the allotted names and another player calls out 'Snap', he or she scores one point. But if the name called out is one of the 'ringers' and anyone shouts 'Snap', that player loses two points. The secret of the game is to call out the names at short intervals, leaving the players little time for thought or to draw breath. Soon chaos will reign supreme, not least with the poor soul who has been given the job of keeping track of the scores.

Rhyme and Reason

Players: Any number

The idea of this game is to establish a chain of rhyming words. The first player thinks of a word which has plenty of possible rhymes, such as 'gate'. He or she then gives a short definition although the word that is being defined is not 'gate' but another word which rhymes with it. The next player has 30 seconds to work out that word and to give a definition for another rhyming word. Any player unable to solve the riddle or to think of a new rhyming word is eliminated. Here is an example of how the game works:

> Player 1: A gate is something you go on with a girlfriend.
>
> Player 2: No, you mean date, which you put on the end of a fishing rod.
>
> Player 3: No, you mean bait, which determines your destiny.
>
> Player 4: No, you mean fate, which is the opposite of early.
>
> Player 5: No, you mean late, which means to dislike intensely.
>
> Player 6: No, you mean hate, which the birds and bees do.
>
> Player 7: No, you mean mate, which you eat dinner off.
>
> Player 8: No, you mean plate, which you measure in kilograms.

And so the game continues until either there is just one player left or until everyone has run out of rhyming words.

Horror Story

Players: Any number

All of the players sit around the fire (even if it's not lit) to tell a horror story. The first player begins a spine-chilling tale, replete with blood-curdling images. As soon as he or she uses an onomatopoeic word (such as creaked or groaned), the next player must take over. The game continues until everyone is too terrified to carry on. Anyone who fails to spot an example of onomatopoeia (a word that sounds like what it describes) must pay a forfeit... like venturing outside alone in the dark.

Fish Market

Players: Any number

Even by the general standard of party games, this one is utterly meaningless and wonderfully silly. Everyone sits in a circle except for one person, the accuser, who is picked to stand in the middle. The others then each announce the name of a fish and the accuser in the middle must try to remember which person is which fish. To disorientate the accuser further, he or she must spin round twice before suddenly jabbing a finger at one of the players in the circle and screaming 'trout, trout, trout' or whatever. The aim is for the accuser to call out the name of the fish three times in quick succession before the player who is that fish can say it once. Should the accuser fail in this mission, as is highly probable, he or she must try again with another player and fish. Should the accuser succeed, he or she swaps places with the trout. There are very few rules to this pastime although any accuser who fails to point at a fish before speaking will have the challenge declared null and void.

Soap Bubbles

Players: Any number

Can you remember which soap opera Alan Turner is in? Or what about Billy Kennedy? Or Simon Raymond? Or Judy Mallett? Here is a quick-fire game for telly addicts in which players are told that every name called out is a character in either *Coronation Street*, *EastEnders*, *Brookside*, *Emmerdale* or *Neighbours*. After the announcement of each name, the first person to call out the correct soap wins a point. In case you have better things to do than watch TV, here are some suitable characters:

Coronation Street: Angie Freeman, Chris Collins, Fred Elliott, Martin Platt, Rita Sullivan, Judy Mallett, Ashley Peacock, Roy Cropper, Deirdre Rachid, Samantha Failsworth, Betty Williams.

EastEnders: Nigel Bates, Lorraine Wicks, Pat Evans, Robbie Jackson, Sarah Hills, Bianca Butcher, Simon Raymond, Sanjay Kapoor, Clare Tyler,

Wellard (Robbie Jackson's dog), Kathy Mitchell, Ruth Fowler.
Brookside: Ron Dixon, Susannah Farnham, Elaine Johnson, Katie Rogers, Ollie Simpson, Sinbad, David Crosbie, Mike Dixon, Julia Brogan, Jackie Corkhill.
Emmerdale: Linda Fowler, Kim Tate, Mandy Dingle, Betty Eagleton, Charlotte Cairns, Seth Armstrong, Alan Turner, Kelly Windsor, Ned Glover, Steve Marchant, Jack Sugden, Eric Pollard.
Neighbours: Billy Kennedy, Lou Carpenter, Madge Bishop, Helen Daniels, Debbie Martin, Darren Starke, Susan Kennedy, Philip Martin, Marlene Kratz.

Get Knotted

Players: Any even number

You will need:
Lengths of string, several pairs of gloves

A team race which will appeal to Boy Scouts and retired Admirals alike. The leader of each team is given a piece of sturdy string, about three feet long. The race starts with the two leaders tying a loose knot in their string which is then passed along the line to their team-mates who also tie knots. The last player in each team takes the knotted string back to the leader who proceeds to untie one knot before passing it on. Each successive team mate unties a knot, the first team to have de-knotted their string completely being the winners. Sounds easy, doesn't it? There's just one thing I forgot to mention — all of the players must wear gloves.

Fancy That!

Players: 8 or more

You will need:
Pencil and paper

This game tests how well you know your fellow guests. One person is elected referee and leaves the room with pencil and paper. The other players in turn give the referee the name of the celebrity they most fancy. It doesn't have to be a particularly strong urge and it certainly doesn't have to have been consummated. Those who are reluctant to reveal their secret longings can always opt for a fictional character such as Desperate Dan or Homer Simpson. Anyway maybe your partner really does fancy Homer Simpson, in which case hide any blue hair dye. When everyone has given a name, the referee returns to the room and reads out the list twice. The players now have to try to work out who fancies who. One player is elected to start and may begin: 'Mildred, I think you fancy Brad Pitt.' Mildred (who has actually listed as her dreamboat John Selwyn Gummer) replies: 'No, but Reginald, I think you fancy Petula Clark.' Mildred has got it in one, at which point Reginald drops out and she moves on to another person. The game ends when everybody has been paired off with their romantic hero.

Spin the Plate

Players: 6 or more

You will need:
Chairs

The guests are seated in chairs arranged in a circle and one player is elected to start. He or she goes to the centre of the circle and is given an old plate, either china or tin, but certainly not the best crockery. The starter spins the plate as vigorously as possible and immediately calls out the name of another player who makes a beeline for the plate. Meanwhile, the starter rushes back to his or her own chair, hoping to sit down before the player whose name has been called out can catch the spinning plate. Should this be the case, the new player takes over as starter and spins the plate before calling out another name. If, however, the starter doesn't sit down in time, he or she must remain in that role, spin the plate again and call for another player. Each player who catches the spinning plate before the starter has sat down in his or her own chair scores five points. With a lot of dashing about and jumping up and down, this is a somewhat frenetic game, best limited to about 15 minutes before anyone keels over.

Silent Partners

Players: 11 or more

All of the players, except one, pair off with the person they know best — spouse, partner, bank manager etc. The singleton, who has probably been chosen for the role because he or she doesn't have any friends, acts as the Grand Inquisitor. When all of the players are seated, the Inquisitor goes over to one partner of a pair and asks a question. However, it is the other partner who must answer. If the player questioned answers or the partner doesn't, that pair are eliminated from the proceedings. The secret of being a wily Inquisitor is to move swiftly from pair to pair, leaving no time for a gathering of wits, and

to think up questions which you know the person you're asking is desperate to answer, but which the partner is equally anxious to avoid. For example, faced with a wife who is an expert secretary and a husband who thinks Pitman's shorthand is a mining injury, you may choose to ask her about the merits of Tipp-Ex. Her natural reaction will be to blurt out the answer, but it is he who must respond. Or you may be confronted with a man with a huge spot on the end of his nose and a woman with a beautifully clear complexion. The obvious, if horribly embarrassing, question to the man would be: 'Does that spot on the end of your nose really hurt?' Yet it is she who is obliged to answer. A breakdown in communications between pairs, resulting in premature elimination, has been known to lead to acrimonious scenes in the car on the way home.

Mouth-to-Mouth

Players: 8 or more

You will need:
Spoons, table tennis balls

This game is best played as a team contest. The players stand in lines and are each given a spoon which they hold between their teeth. The team leaders are each provided with a table tennis ball which is placed on their spoon. The ball is then passed down the line from spoon to spoon, the first team to transport the ball from end of the line to the other being the winner. At no time may hands be used. Even if the ball is dropped, it can only be picked up by a spoon in the mouth. If you don't have access to table tennis balls, you can use peanuts or grapes instead. But don't use anything too heavy — it might rattle your dentures.

Paper Models

Players: Any even number

You will need:
Newspapers, pins

Using sheets of newspaper, pairs of players each attempt to create a sensational new dress in five minutes, joining the different pages together with pins. Each pair are given the same number of sheets of paper and the same number of pins with one player serving as the model while the other acts as dressmaker. Holes can be made to accommodate arms and, if so desired, the designer may even run to a matching hat. The pair who create what is judged to be the best outfit win the game.

Animal Snap

Players: 3-6

You will need:
A pack of playing cards

Deal a pack of cards among all of the players who reveal that, henceforth, they will behave in the manner of a goat, pig, sheep or whichever animal takes their fancy. It's worth discouraging anyone from being a lemming as they tend to have a tendency to throw themselves out of the nearest window. The game then proceeds like 'Snap' except that whenever two cards are matched, instead of shouting 'Snap!', the players must make the animal noise of the player who lays the matching (the second) card, regardless of whether or not it is their own. Thus, the air resounds to a chorus of moos or oinks in a manic free-for-all. The first player to make the correct noise wins the cards on offer. Any player able to make the sounds of both animals involved before anyone else is able to grunt or squeak automatically wins 10 cards. As with the more conventional version of 'Snap', the winner is the player who acquires the whole pack.

Slave Auction

Players: 10 or more

You will need:
Coins

This may not be the most politically correct of party games but with the right company, it can be one of the most entertaining. Half-a-dozen or so players are taken to one side and put up for auction. The rest are given an equal number of coins, say 20, and are instructed to buy as many slaves as possible. To keep any objections to a minimum, select both male and female slaves. The host acts as auctioneer and presents a colourful sales pitch to encourage bidding for the first slave. 'Slim, shapely legs, lovely silky hair, gorgeous figure, 'come-to-bed' eyes, so if anyone wants to buy Mr. Pettigrew, the bidding starts at 2p.' The bidders meanwhile try to urge each other to pay over the odds, knowing that once their rivals have run out of coins, there'll be the opportunity to snap up bargains. The canny bidder watches others making panic buys while retaining his or her own coins for the later lots. At the end of the auction, the player who has purchased the greatest number of slaves wins. If it is a tie, whoever has most coins left wins. And then the players can do whatever they want with their slaves... at least, that's the theory.

Clip Together

Players: Any even number

You will need:
Paper clips, chairs

Split the participants into two teams and seat them facing each other in rows. Give each player a paper clip to be held behind the back. At the off, the first player in each team passes his or her clip to the next person in line who hooks it onto his or her own and passes both clips to the third team member. The ever-growing chain continues in this way until it reaches the end of the line from where it is ferried back to the first person, this time in front of the players, and solely by means of the elbows. Once back with player one, he or she puts the chain behind his or her back, unhooks one clip and passes the rest on down the line, each successive player unhooking a clip. When all of the members of one team are each able to hold up a paper clip, that team is victorious.

My Little Bird

Players: Any number

Everyone sits in a circle and one player is elected to be the leader. This individual begins by announcing: 'My little bird is lively' and then adds something followed by the word 'fly', maybe 'cuckoos fly'. If the object that is named can fly, the other players wave their arms around in the air and jump up and down making squawking sounds. If, however, the object named can't fly — like penguins, ostriches or gas cookers — the remaining players must remain absolutely still. Anyone who gets it wrong is eliminated, the last player left in wins the game. Apart from flightless birds, the trick is to put in things like lizards, squirrels and fish, all of which have species which can fly.

Alliteration

Players: 4-8

Another circular game where players have to remember and recite an ever-lengthening alliterative list. The first player thinks up a two-word alliteration beginning with 'O' and says something along the lines of: 'One organised okapi.' The next player might weigh in with: 'Two terrifying terrapins and one organised okapi.' By player three, the alliteration has extended by an additional word so the offering might be: 'Three thin, thoughtful thrushes, two terrifying terrapins and one organised okapi.' And so it goes on with each successive player adding a word to make an alliterative list matching the number at the start — such as 'four fat, fiendish, furry felines' — as well as reciting the previous offerings. Anyone who blunders is out, the last person left in being the winner.

Dinner Party

Players: 4-8

You will need:
Pencils and paper

It's every dinner party hostess's nightmare. In an effort to invite a representative cross-section of guests, she has merely succeeded in bringing together six people who have absolutely nothing in common and thus have nothing whatsoever to say to each other. For this game, each player must think up a list of six party guests who would be a disaster seated around the same table simply because they would have nothing in common. The guests can be dead or alive, real or fictional. Then, confronted with one list at a time, the other players must try to argue why some of the six would be able to engage in conversation. So while a list comprising William the Conqueror, Judith Chalmers, Bugs Bunny, Vincent Van Gogh, Sir Francis Drake and George Stephenson would appear, at first glance, to have no connections, it could be argued that Bugs Bunny would tell Van Gogh: 'That's not how you draw a carrot', George Stephenson would tell William the Conqueror how his invention has speeded up cross-Channel travel, and Sir Francis Drake would show Judith Chalmers his holiday snaps of Spain. And for good measure, Judith would point out to William that he and the Norman army would have found the journey more economical if they'd travelled Dieppe-Newhaven on a Weekday Return.

Tissue Trail

Players: Any even number

You will need:
Drinking straws, paper tissues

Players split into two teams and place a drinking straw in their mouth. The team leaders put a paper tissue over the end of their straw and suck in, thereby ensuring that it is held in place. They then turn to the next players in line and pass the tissue on to them, the secret of success being for the first player to breathe out gently at the same time as the second player sucks in. Following this method, the tissue is passed along the entire team, the first team to finish winning the game. Other than at the very start, the only time the tissue may be handled is if it floats to the floor when it may be picked up and returned to its position at the end of the straw.

Bean Feast

Players: 3-6

You will need:
Bowls, baked beans, sweets, plastic sheets

This is a messy game, so much so that it is a good idea to cover your floor with plastic sheets. Each player is confronted with a deep bowl filled with baked beans, buried at the bottom of which is a sweet still in its wrapper. On the command 'Go!' and using only their teeth, contestants must burrow nose first into the morass of baked beans and pull out the sweet with their teeth, the first do so being the winner. Obviously, the deeper the bowl, the more fun the game. And if you don't want to use baked beans, you can always substitute mushy peas or, for a less mucky contest, cornflakes.

Name Calling

Players: Any number

This game tests players' ability to think against the background of a relentless jungle beat. Everyone sits around the table and sets up a continuous rhythm of clapping hands twice and banging on the table twice. On the second bang, the leader calls out the name of a category — say, jockeys — and on the next second bang, the first player shouts out a suitable example, maybe Frankie Dettori. The incessant rhythm must be maintained throughout and players must only answer on the second bang. Anyone who loses rhythm, answers at the wrong time or can't think of a reply, loses one of their three lives. The categories can be changed whenever a particular line has been exhausted. Interesting categories include: sex symbols, rock bands beginning with S, items of clothing and, if it really is getting late, swear words.

Mystery Maxims

Players: 4-8

One member of the group is sent from the room while the remainder decide upon a proverb. When the absentee returns, each of the other players in turn speaks a sentence which includes one of the words contained in the chosen proverb, and in the correct order. So the first sentence must contain the first word of the proverb, the second sentence the second word and so on. If the chosen proverb is 'Too many cooks spoil the broth', the statements could go:

1. Many gourmets are not too keen on custard.
2. To save time in the kitchen, many people use electrical gadgets instead of their hands.
3. I have seen cooks make excellent soufflés.
4. But they can spoil unless they are really light.
5. The work in a restaurant kitchen is extremely hard.
6. On a cold winter's day, you can't beat a good broth.

'Broth' is probably the giveaway, but until then there was also the possibility that the proverb could have been 'Many hands make light work'. If the player guesses the proverb following the first sentence (and only three guesses are allowed in total), six points are scored, after the second sentence five, and so on with decreasing value. When the answer has been revealed, it is the turn of someone else to leave the room. This game can be played equally well with song titles or film titles.

The Forbidden Fruit

Players: Any number

You will need:
An envelope, a piece of paper

This game involves the entire party. At some stage in the proceedings, the host holds up a sealed envelope and says that it is a forbidden fruit and that whoever has possession of the envelope when it is time to go home is forced to perform the final forfeit of the evening which is written on a piece of paper inside. So from the moment of the host's announcement, everyone is on their guard in case someone slips them the forbidden fruit. Whenever this happens, the person offloading the envelope into a pocket, handbag or whatever, must whisper to the victim that somewhere about their person is the forbidden fruit. The victim in turn tries to pass it on but must take care not to be caught in the act, the punishment for such a crime being a forfeit. Alternatively, the game can be played using two envelopes — one containing a forfeit, the other a prize. So when the guests are told they've got the forbidden fruit, they are in a dilemma as to whether to keep it or pass it on.

Woolly Tangle

Players: 3-6

You will need:
Chairs, balls of wool

Using one chair per player, wrap a ball of wool around the arms, legs and back of each chair so that it is in a total tangle. While remaining seated in their chairs at all times, the players must untangle the strands as quickly as possible and roll them back into a recognisable ball. The first player able to do so wins the game.

Blow-Out

Players: Any even number

You will need:
Candles, blindfolds

Two lit candles are placed on a table in the centre of the room, about eight inches apart. The players are divided into teams starting from diagonally opposite corners of the room with their backs to the candles. The first player in each team is blindfolded and they make their way towards the table with the intention of blowing out their candle only. The candle for each competitor is the one on their right. If a player happens to blow out the wrong candle, victory goes to the opposing team. In a bid to prevent this, the next in line on both teams can issue instructions, but only five words may be used — 'Left', 'Right', 'Up', 'Down' and 'Blow'. If matters get out of hand, a sixth word may be used — 'Fire!' After the candle has been blown out, the remaining team members have a go in turn, the eventual winners being the team with most successful blows and who still have all of their eyebrows. To minimise the chances of any singeing, one guest should be stationed at the table at all times.

Nelson's Eye

Players: 6 or more

You will need:
A chair, a stuffed stocking, a marble, an over-ripe strawberry, blindfolds

There are certain things you only want to do once in your life — like sit your A' Levels, get married, take your driving test or drink sherry. Playing 'Nelson's Eye' definitely comes into that category. For that reason, when choosing volunteers to take part, it's essential to ascertain that they're not familiar with the game. The four or so volunteers are led out of the room and brought back in blindfolded, one at a time. One of the other players immediately asks the blind man to 'feel Nelson's good leg', and the blind man's hands are guided so that he can feel someone's leg. He's then asked to feel Nelson's bad leg, and his hands are steered to a chair leg. So far, so good. Next the blind man is told to feel Nelson's good arm and his hands are guided to someone's arm. Then he must feel Nelson's bad arm whereupon he finds himself groping a stuffed stocking. This is followed by Nelson's good eye, at which he is presented with a marble. Finally, he's asked to feel Nelson's bad eye and finds his fingers sinking into a squashy, over-ripe strawberry! At this point, there's usually a cry of anguish... and a vow never to be caught out again.

Happy Families

Players: Groups of 3

You will need:
Pieces of paper

Before the game, write on separate slips of paper various animal families — mother, father and baby. The creatures should be chosen on the basis of being difficult to impersonate — like rhinoceros, hamster, stick insect. Gather the players around and distribute the pieces of paper among them at random. When play begins, each animal must try to find the rest of its family, solely by making the noise of that animal and by mimicking its movements. No human words may be spoken. So baby chipmunk will be scurrying around frantically, perhaps pausing for the occasional imaginary nut, in search of mother and father chipmunk. When all three have been reunited, the mother sits in a chair with the baby on her lap and the father behind her. This can create an interesting spectacle if the baby is played by a weightlifter and the mother by a hairdresser. The first group to line up like this wins the game although proceedings continue until the very last family — invariably the snails — are together. If you find yourself as a member of the mayfly family, don't take too long over this game.

Pick-Me-Up

Players: 3-6

You will need:
Rice, gardening gloves, small bottles

This is a game requiring remarkable dexterity, a commodity which will almost certainly be at a premium at this stage of the evening. Each player puts on a gardening glove (or something similar) and, using only the gloved hand, has to transfer grains of rice from a table-top pile into a small, narrow-necked bottle. Furthermore, he or she must only transfer one grain at a time. Judges will be

on hand to ensure fair play. Whoever has the most legally-acquired grains of rice in his or her bottle at the end of three minutes is the winner.

Bah Humbug!

Players: 4-8

This fast-moving word game is played like a tennis match around a table by two teams of up to four players on each side. One player on the serving team looks at a player on the opposite side and serves a word, at the same time beginning a tapping rhythm on the table which everybody else emulates. The word must be returned by the chosen player before the fourth tap and must either rhyme with or begin with the same letter as the served word. The only exception is any word starting with B which must be answered instead by 'Bah Humbug!' before play continues as previously. A player must always look at the opponent to whom he or she is hitting the ball. Failure to meet any of these requirements results in the loss of the rally, scoring being the same as in tennis. A typical rally might go: Jog, Dog, Dandruff, Dromedary, Dyke, Hike, Like, Limpet, Listen, Glisten, Grab, Gale, Hail, Bail, Bah Humbug! Mail, Mastodon, Medium, Tedium, Trip, Drip, Grip, Nip, Nothing, Never, Nuance, Nightingale, panic, panic, love-15.

Apple on a String

Players: 3-6

You will need:
Apples, lengths of string

For this old Halloween party favourite, you need to suspend from the ceiling a length of string for each player and to the end of each piece of string tie an apple. The apples should be above head height, but within mouth reach of the participants. At the off, the players must munch into their dangling apples without using their hands. The first player to get down to the core is the winner.

Happy Travellers

Players: Any even number

You will need:
Newspapers, chairs

This jolly little pastime recreates the perils of trying to read a broadsheet newspaper on the London Underground in rush hour, an activity which has been known to result in the loss of eyes, teeth and wallets. Two teams sit facing each other in rows, the team-mates so close together that their knees are touching. All are given copies of the same newspaper, the pages of which have been hopelessly muddled up. The first team to get all of their newspapers in the right order win. So that the flank players don't have the unfair advantage of extra elbow room, non-contestants should sit on the ends of the rows.

Running Flush

Players: 12 or more

You will need:
A pack of playing cards

If you have 52 guests at a party — plus two jokers — this is the ideal game, reminiscent of all those student attempts to cram as many people as possible into a phone box. But even with smaller numbers, it can still be great fun and none-too taxing on the brain cells. In the event of there being 20 players, you need to take a pack of cards and remove all of the aces, kings, queens, jacks and 10s. Shuffle those 20 cards and deal them out face down on the floor (the cards, not you). Each player races forward to grab a card and the four who end up with the aces call out the name of their suit and speed to the nearest chair. The other four players with cards of the same suit run over to their ace and sit down in formation. The ace sits on the chair, the king sits on the ace's lap, the queen sits on the king's lap, the jack sits on the queen's lap and the 10 perches, somewhat precariously by now, on the jack's lap. The first suit to get every player in position wins. At this point, it is worth establishing whether any of the aces suffer from weak hearts.

Tales of the Riverbank

Players: 3-6

You will need:
Paper clips, wire coathangers, a washing-up bowl

Fill a large washing-up bowl with water and empty a box of paper clips into the bottom. Each player kneels around the bowl wielding a length of wire which has been bent at one end to produce a hook. Wire coathangers can be straightened out to make acceptable fishing rods. On the command 'Go!', the anglers try to hook the paper clips amid a frenzy of activity which would scare off Jaws. When all the clips have been hooked, the player who has caught the most is declared the champion fisherman... while the rest get to talk about the paper clip that got away.

Tunnel Ball

Players: Any even number

You will need:
Balloons, blindfolds

Who would think that you could have so much fun with a balloon? Well, here's another simple game guaranteed to provide mirth and merriment for all but direct descendants of Oliver Cromwell. Two teams line up blindfolded with their heads down and their legs apart. This position may be familiar to those of you who have read back copies of *Mayfair* at the dentist. The first player in each team has a balloon and must pass it back between his or her legs to the next player. With everyone groping around in the dark, the balloon must continue its passage in this way until it reaches the end of the line. The first team to get the balloon through the last pair of legs wins the game.

Dictation

Players: Any even number

You will need:
Newspaper cuttings, pencils and paper

An equal number of bosses and secretaries line up on opposite sides of a table. Be sure that each secretary knows who is his or her boss and vice-versa but then arrange the seating so that no pair are opposite each other — in fact the further away they are, the better. Each boss is supplied with a different newspaper story of approximately the same length which she or he will endeavour to dictate to his trusty secretary, armed with pencil and notepad (or paper). All bosses begin dictating their different stories at the same time so it quickly becomes a nightmare for the poor secretary straining to hear her boss's words above all the others. To add to the confusion, arrange for the volume on the office radio to be turned up half-way through. At the end of the dictation, compare the secretaries' versions with the original newspaper stories. Any similarity will probably be purely coincidental.

Conversation Stoppers

Players: Any number

Two players agree privately on a word. Without mentioning the word itself, they strike up a conversation, dropping clues here and there. As other members of the ensemble decide that they know the word, they join in the conversation and try to prove to the pair, again without saying the actual word, that they know what it is. If it becomes clear that they don't, they have to turn their back on the company. There are no winners, but the last person to enter the conversation is judged to be thick and is given a forfeit. The best words to choose are ones with a double meaning such as 'back', 'crane' or 'ball'. That way, you can mislead the other players with a veritable shoal of red herrings.

Feathers

Players: Any number

You will need:
A feather

With the players lying on their backs on the floor, throw a feather into the air. Everyone must do their utmost to prevent the feather landing on them, blowing frantically to force it in another direction. Players may move their head for the purposes of blowing, but no other part of their body. Whoever the feather lands on is out. The last person left in is the winner.

Artist, Composer, Writer

Players: Any number

Draw up a list of well-known artists, composers and writers and call them out one at a time. The first person who answers correctly 'artist', 'composer' or 'writer' to each name earns a point. To confuse matters, slip in a few miscellaneous historical figures who don't fit into any of the three categories. Players who shout out 'artist', 'composer' or 'writer' to any of these names lose a point. At the end of the game, the winner is the player with the highest total. Here are some suitable examples:

Artists: Caravaggio, Chardin, Memling, Tintoretto, Angelico, Degas, Bellini, Fragonard, Botticelli, Correggio.

Composers: Puccini, Rossini, Webern, Gluck, Berlioz, Delius, Sousa, Glinka, Mahler, Rameau.

Writers: Boccaccio, Sheridan, Wieland, Baudelaire, France, Dostoevsky, Gautier, Pirandello, Rimbaud, Verlaine.

Others: Fellini (film director), Artaud (theatre director), Bolivar (Venezuelan revolutionary leader), Daguerre (scientist), Galvani (doctor), Rasmussen (explorer).

Guzzle Grand Prix

Players: 3-6

You will need:
Bowls, tea spoons

Here is the ideal sobering-up game after a surfeit of wine. Each player must drink a large bowl of water, using only a tea spoon, the first to scoop up every last drop feeling not only victorious but sufficiently invigorated to tackle another bottle of wine.

The Prince of Wales Has Lost His Hat

Players: 6 or more

This game can seem positively baffling when everyone is sober, so if your guests have had a few to drink it is a recipe for total chaos. The players sit around a table and are numbered according to the amount of participants. Player one declares: 'The Prince of Wales has lost his hat' and adds that one of the others (say, number four) has found it. Number four immediately replies: 'No, sir. Not I, sir.' 'Then who, sir?' demands number one. 'Two, sir,' suggests number four. But player two counters: 'No, sir. Not I sir.' 'Then who, sir?' asks player four. 'Five, sir,' says player two. And so the round of questions and answers continues, gathering pace all the time. Anyone who gets the words wrong moves to the end chair (with eight players, this would be number eight) and the numbers change accordingly. Therefore, if number one made a mistake, he or she would then become number eight, eight would become seven, seven would become six, six would become five, five would become four, four would become three, three would become two and two would become one! So when you contemplate playing this game, don't say you weren't warned.

Pass the Polo

Players: Any even number

You will need:
Cocktail sticks, Polo mints

The players line up as two teams with cocktail sticks between their teeth. The first player in each team has a Polo mint balanced near the end of his or her stick. The object of the game is to pass the Polo down the line from stick to stick without using hands, the first team to reach the other end being the winner. If a mint is dropped at any stage, the offending team has to go right back to the start. While calculating the right angle at the takeover point, players should refrain from stabbing their team mate with the stick.

The Balloon Game

Players: 3-6

The Balloon Game represents the ultimate test of historical importance. Three famous people are flying in a balloon when the contraption springs a leak. The decision is: which of the three should be sacrificed by being jettisoned over the side so that the other two can be saved? The game begins with each player (or pair) choosing an occupant. The trio should be as diverse as possible to encourage lively debate. A good mixture might be Max Bygraves, Grace Darling and Judge Jeffreys. The latter might seem the obvious candidate for expulsion on the strength of mercilessly ordering the execution of 320 rebels in the 17th century, until you remember all those Singalong-a-Max albums. And there could be different grounds for throwing out someone like Henry VIII or Pavarotti, simply because the weight loss would enable the balloon to stay airborne a little longer. Any decision should be debated at length and then a vote taken to decide who goes. Of course, if the occupants were Michael Portillo, Edd the Duck and Gazza, the game would be simple. You'd just throw the lot of them out.

The Laughing Handkerchief

Players: Any number

You will need:
A handkerchief

Party games don't come much dafter than this. One person stands in the middle of the room with a handkerchief (preferably clean) and the other players are positioned in a circle around the outside. When he or she lets go of the handkerchief, that is the signal for everyone else to start laughing like hyenas. But the moment it touches the floor, they must stop. Anyone who fails to laugh for the duration of the handkerchief's descent or who continues laughing after it has landed, is eliminated. The last player left in wins the prize — a jar of Michelle Pfeiffer's snot for the boys, and Charlie Sheen's for the girls.

I Wish...

Players: Any number

The players sit in a circle and think of the character, fact or fiction, dead or alive, that they would most like to be. Then the first player states: 'I wish I had been Sir Walter Raleigh' or whoever he chooses. Then he has to explain why — perhaps that when he threw down his coat, he would have got a good view of Queen Elizabeth's legs or that he would have been proud to have introduced the potato to Europe. The eventual winner is the person who gives the best reasons for his or her choice of alter-ego.

Catch the Cane

Players: Any number

You will need:
A stick or cane, chairs

Assign each player the name of a town and hand the list of towns to the person who has been elected cane master. While the players sit in a circle of chairs, the cane master stands in the middle, brandishing a stick or garden cane. Lifting his or her fingers from the stick, the cane master calls out the name of a town whose owner must somehow catch the stick before it hits the floor. Failure to do so results in elimination; success means that player takes over in the middle. The faster the game is played, the more fun it is.

Chinese Puzzle

Players: 6 or more

While one player leaves the room, the rest join hands in a circle and, without letting go, arrange themselves into a twisted mass of bodies. This is achieved by ducking under arms, stepping over arms, putting heads through legs and generally climbing over or under each other. Then everyone shuffles, crawls or edges closer together like a giant knot with heads, arms and feet protruding from the most unlikely orifices. You can discover parts of people's bodies you never knew existed. Finally, the singleton returns and tries to unravel the mess, the aim being to return the players to the original circle shape without loosening any of their hands. However, he or she may find that some players have become very attached to each other.

Needle and Cork

Players: 4-8

You will need:
Washing-up bowl, corks, darning needles

Float a number of corks in a washing-up bowl full of water (make sure there are at least three times as many corks as players) and supply each player with a darning needle. They then have to lift the corks out of the water by spiking them with their needles. The player who has recovered most corks in two minutes is the winner.

Quick Clues

Players: Any even number

You will need:
Slips of paper, pencils, a hat or bowl

All of the players pair off and each person thinks of two similar items — rock stars, movie stars, TV stars, film titles, book titles, TV programmes, artists, authors, statesmen, sportsmen and so on. Each idea is written down on a separate slip of paper, folded over and placed in a hat, bowl or some other form of container. One partner then picks a slip of paper at random and has two minutes in which to describe to his or her partner what is written on the paper without using any of the actual words. If the partner guesses correctly, they move on to another slip, the pair who solve the most puzzles in their allotted two minutes emerging as the winners. The key to success is to deliver short, sharp clues which do everything but mention the words on the paper. For instance, if you had to describe 'Elton John', you might say, 'Rocket Man. Plays the piano. Big glasses. Colourful clothes. Silly haircut. Supports Watford, for God's sake...' If your partner suggests Reg Holdsworth, you might as well cut your losses and go home.

Mat Finish

Players: Any even number

You will need:
Beer mats, chairs

Two teams line up sitting on chairs facing each other. At one end of each team, the respective captains sit with a pile of six beer mats on their knee. At the off, the captain picks up one of the mats and holds it at the top and bottom between the tips of his or her forefingers. The mat is moved towards the player on the captain's left. The captain removes his or her top finger, which is replaced by the second player's left finger. Together they turn the mat over and the captain removes his or her lower finger, to be replaced by the second player's right finger. This procedure is repeated along the line until the mat is perched on the last player's knee. That player then calls out 'Next!' and the second mat begins its journey. The first team to get six beer mats on the last player's knee wins the game. Any dropped mat has to go back to the captain who starts that 'leg' of the relay again.

Spoons

Players: 6-12

You will need:
A pack of playing cards, spoons

The players sit on the floor in a circle in the middle of which is a pile of spoons, one less than the number of players. From the pack of cards, select four cards of a kind for each player. So if there are seven players, you need to use 28 cards — four aces, four kings, four queens, four jacks, four 10s, four nines and four eights. The cards are shuffled and dealt to the players. If nobody has four of a kind (such as four aces), they all pass one card to their left simultaneously. They continue passing cards (always at the same time) until one player gets four of a kind. As soon as that happens, that player stops passing and grabs a spoon. This alerts the others who also dive into the middle to snatch a spoon. However, since there is one spoon short, one player is unlucky and is eliminated from the game. Before play resumes, another spoon is removed and the action continues, a bit like musical chairs, until there are just two card players competing for one spoon. As the tension reaches breaking point, whoever gets four of a kind snatches the final spoon in triumph... and probably embarks on a lap of honour around the sofa.

Conked Out

Players: Any even number

You will need:
Matchboxes

If you have a nose which puts Cyrano de Bergerac, and indeed large areas of the Cotswolds, in the shade, here at last is an activity at which your huge hooter may shine. For at 'Conked Out', a long nose has a distinct advantage

over squat, flat, pug-noses. Players line up as two teams. The team leader pushes the cover of a matchbox on to his or her nose and tries to transfer it to the proboscis of the next player without using any hands. The matchbox proceeds in this manner down the line, with the first team to switch it right from one end to the other, solely via snouts, being the winner. If any player drops the matchbox or inadvertently touches it by hand, that team has to start all over again. It may seem a harsh penalty, but this isn't a game for wimps.

Tell the Truth

Players: Any number

You will need:
Pencils and paper

Each player has to write down five supposed facts about himself or herself, of which only one is true. The other players then have to try to decide which is the true fact. Obviously if your life-long partner is among your fellow players, you'll need to dredge up something pretty obscure, but most people have some hidden secret, no matter how trivial. The important thing is not to make the genuine truth stand out like a sore thumb — your invented answers must be equally plausible. It won't take a genius to work out your true fact if your five suggestions are:

1. I once knocked out Mike Tyson, but nobody was watching
2. I once climbed Everest before lunch
3. I once stood in for President Clinton at a world summit
4. I once gave Demi Moore a tongue-sandwich
5. I once spotted 16 different makes of locomotive on Crewe station in 33 minutes

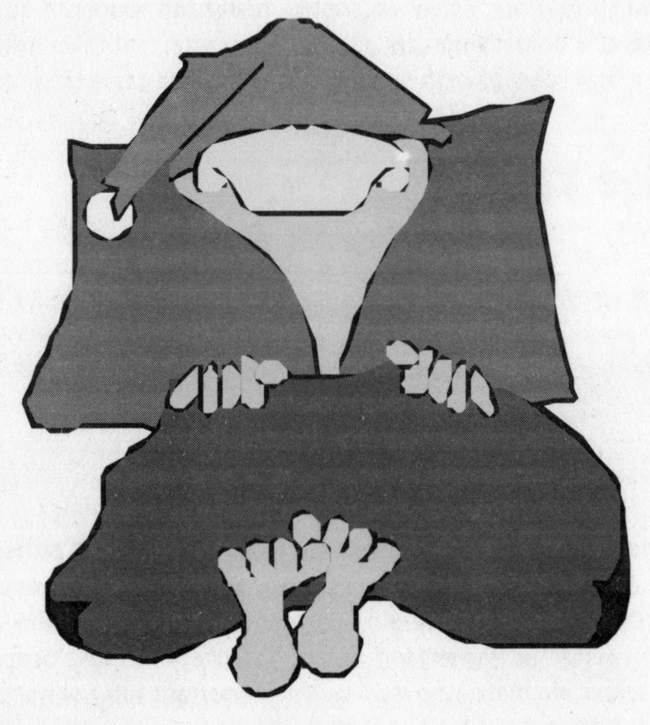

TIME FOR BED

The Psychiatrist's Couch

Players: Any number

You will need:
A sofa

After conversation and wine have been flowing in equal measures for several hours, why shouldn't you round off a memorable evening with a spot of psychoanalysis? The reason why not is because some of your answers may come back to haunt you. So be warned — don't volunteer to be a patient in this game if your tongue is loose. The chosen patient lies down on the sofa and is subjected to 10 minutes of intense questioning by the other players who act as psychiatrists. You'll get their bill later. The patient is told to answer all questions truthfully and at the end of the session, the psychiatrists analyse his or her problems, sometimes painfully. While the patient squirms at the diagnoses, he or she may even hear the odd grain of truth, however unwelcome. The psychiatrist whose evaluation turns out to be the most accurate wins the game. Then it is someone else's turn to lie on the couch — if anyone is mad enough or drunk enough.

Analogies

Players: Any number

This is another game best played when everyone is plastered, simply in the hope that by the next day nobody will remember what was said. One person at a time is chosen from the gathering to be the subject of a series of analogies. The categories should be as wide-ranging as possible. For example in the case of someone called Tim, the questioning could go:

If Tim was a breed of dog, what sort would he be?
If Tim was a vegetable, would sort he be?
If Tim was a means of transport, what sort would he be?
If Tim was a film, what title would he be?

If Tim was a drink, what sort would he be?

And if Tim was a household item, what would he be?

If, after much debate, the general consensus of opinion is that Tim would be a toy poodle, a cabbage, a Sinclair C5, Bambi, Horlicks and a potato peeler, Tim would probably want the ground to open up and swallow him. However, if Tim were to emerge as a great dane, a fine sturdy carrot, a Harley Davidson, Terminator 2, Drambuie and the latest hi-fi, Tim would probably sleep contentedly that night. So it pays to be nice to your friends.

Personality Change

Players: Any even number

Another potentially dangerous game, this requires two partners to exchange personalities for five minutes at a time and behave in the manner in which they think their partner would behave. If this is a first date, it can bring a swift end to a relationship. Yet it can be even more devastating on a couple who've been together for years but who've kept silent until now about things their partner does which irritate them. So if you cruelly embarrass your wife by telling everyone present that she clips her toenails at the dinner table — usually during the soup course — expect an equally rough ride when it is her turn to lay into you.

Jump!

Players: 4 plus an audience

You will need:
A stool, a blindfold, a book

A victim is blindfolded and seated on a high stool. Two strong players stand in front of the stool, one at either side, and allow the victim to put his hands on their shoulders. Holding the stool by the legs, they then lift it a couple of inches off the ground and at the same time another player taps the victim's head firmly with a hard-backed book. Disorientated by the blindfold — and probably a considerable intake of alcohol — he's now convinced that the bump on the head was the ceiling and that the stool is way off the ground. Meanwhile, the two supporters gently sink to their knees, lower the stool imperceptibly to terra firma and creep away. The onlookers start urging the victim to jump but, thinking he's still floating in mid-air, will more likely appear absolutely terrified. It's a mean trick and should be played on someone who deserves to be made to look stupid.

Tongue-Twisters

Players: Any number

When everyone's too tired for a game requiring too much effort, slip in a few tongue-twisters. The beauty of this game as a late-night activity is that it can be played from wherever the participants happen to be at the time — flat out on the sofa, underneath the kitchen table or even hanging from the curtains. So test sobriety with 'The Leith police dismisseth us', 'Red lorry, yellow lorry', 'Sister Suzie sews silver shirts for soldiers' and 'The sixth sick sheik's sixth sheep's sick.' If there are ladies present, it might be best to avoid any reference to pheasant pluckers.

Slander!

Players: Any number

Here is an opportunity to get rid of all the bitterness and resentment which you may feel towards certain over-rated, over-paid celebrities. Each player picks a famous person to slander and proceeds to tear him or her to shreds with a succession of vicious barbs, all the while avoiding any mention of the victim's name. The other players simply have to guess who is on the receiving end of such venom. On no account should any attempt be made to play this game using fellow guests as victims instead of celebrities... unless you're emigrating to South America the following day.

All True

Players: Any number

This is not a game to enter into lightly. For all players must promise to speak the truth, the whole truth and nothing but the truth for its duration. That may sound innocuous enough for questions like: 'What's your favourite root vegetable?' But some guests will want to delve deeper and may ask: 'What's the worst lie you've ever told?' 'Have you ever been dishonest?' 'Have you ever had an affair?' And that is probably when you decide to forget about the rules and conclude that discretion is definitely the better part of valour.

Russian Omelette

Players: 3-8

You will need:
Eggs

This non-fatal version of Russian roulette leaves the victim with nothing more than wounded pride. The day before the party, you need to hard boil a number of eggs — one fewer than there will be players. For the game itself, seat everyone around a table and introduce a raw egg among the hard-boiled ones. Only you will know which is the raw one so if there's one particular guest that you want to see end up with egg on their face, place it in front of that person. If he or she subsequently complains about being singled out you can, of course, insist that you had no idea which was the raw egg. Even if you don't have anybody in mind to be the victim, make sure that the raw egg is not one of the first to be cracked because that rather spoils the fun. One by one, the players are told to crack their egg on top of their head. The relief is almost tangible as player after player emerges from the ordeal unscathed, but among those still to come the tension is unbearable, broken only when a rivulet of egg finally trickles down their face.

One-Minute walk

Players: Any number

You will need:
A watch

Cover all the clocks, confiscate all watches and egg-timers and tell the players they must walk from one end of the room in exactly a minute. They all start together and must maintain constant movement and adhere to an even pace. Anyone found guilty of stopping, even for a split second, or who reaches the finish too soon is eliminated. When 60 seconds are up, the host calls out 'Stop!' and whoever's nearest the finish line at that moment is declared the winner.

Toddlers

Players: Any number

You will need:
Children's toys

For all the clever word games and inventive activities you come up with, don't be surprised if the most popular game at your party turns out to be one where grown-ups get the chance to revert to childhood. Tell your guests that, for 15 heavenly minutes, they are to go back to being three-year-olds and so there should be plenty of pushing and shoving, pulling and tugging and temper tantrums. It is essential to stipulate that the players behave as toddlers and not babies because then you won't have to change any nappies. If available, toys can be provided to be hurled around the room. You may even go as far as to dish out some jelly and ice cream, but this is only advisable if you intend re-decorating. And don't forget to hide the cat.

Beauty Queen

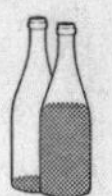

Players: Any number

You will need:
Pencils and paper

Don't worry, this isn't as tacky as it sounds. Instead it is a send-up of all those insincere beauty contest speeches where the contestants declare that they would like to 'travel, meet people, help little old ladies across the road and end world famine.' Each player is given a beauty queen title — 'Miss Nomer', 'Miss Place', 'Miss Chief' — and has to write down three things which he or she would like to do. These should be as ridiculous and pretentious as possible — such as 'rewrite Einstein's Theory of Relativity, discover a cure for hereditary flatulence and get my roots done.' The player who comes up with the wildest, wittiest or weirdest suggestions is crowned the overall Party Queen.

Gurning

Players: Any number

The ancient Cumbrian sport of gurning (where competitors have to pull the most hideous face imaginable) makes an admirable party game for that time of night when guests are no longer able to summon the power of speech. Simply imagine that someone has substituted vinegar for Coca-Cola and envisage the face you would pull as a result of drinking a glass. However, if it's been a good party the face you look at in the bathroom mirror the next morning may be only a marginal improvement.

My Best Friend

Players: Any number

At the end of a drunken evening, it's not uncommon for men to get exceedingly maudlin and grant whoever they happen to be with the accolade of being 'my best friend', even if they only met him an hour earlier. For this game, one male player sets the ball rolling by telling everyone else: 'You're my best friend.' In turn, the others (male and female) have to say why he is their best friend, too, but the answer they give must be a song title. Reasons for best mate-dom could therefore include:

Player One: 'You Make Me Feel Brand New'
Player Two: 'You Can Do Magic'
Player Three: 'You Are The Sunshine Of My Life'
Player Four: 'You Make Me Feel Like Dancing'
Player Five: 'You To Me Are Everything'

After a couple of rounds, there won't be a dry eye in the house.

Bunny Rabbits

Players: Any number

Announce to everyone that they're going to play 'Bunny Rabbits'. Get all the bunnies in line close together, stand at the end and tell them to copy whatever you do. First you use your hands to do the bunny's ears and everyone dutifully copies. Then you squat like a bunny and everyone squats with their hands between their legs. Then you hop like a bunny, and, as they hop up and down on the spot, you lean into the bunny next to you and send the whole line toppling like dominoes!

Traumas

Players: Any number

One player leaves the room while the others think of a dreadful traumatic experience for him or her to have undergone at some time in life. It really shouldn't be anything half-hearted like the car breaking down on the way to an important meeting, but something which could leave deep emotional scarring such as discovering that your long-lost father is now known as Anita and lives with a Rugby League prop forward. On returning, the player has 20 questions in which to learn the nature of his or her trauma from the other participants. All questions, however, can only be answered with a 'yes' or a 'no'. When the precise suffering is revealed, someone else has a turn at being traumatised.

If The Cap Fits

Players: Any number

You will need:
Pencils, slips of paper

Each player writes down an adjective to describe someone else in the room. The chosen word should be truthful but not necessarily complimentary. On the top right-hand corner of their slips of paper, the players should write the name of the person to whom the adjective refers. The individual slips are then folded over and handed to the host who reads out the first word. The players then argue over which of them it describes best. Even the person who chose the word joins in, if only to avoid being identified as its author, either through embarrassment or fear, depending on the nature of the adjective. When a consensus of opinion arrives at the most likely name, the host reveals the identity of the guest. If the adjective was too abusive, it might be wise to have the victim's coat ready.

Line Walking

Players: Any number

You will need:
Masking tape, a pair of binoculars

This is the ideal game to play before everyone finds out whether they're sober enough to walk out into the night air. Lay a strip of masking tape in a straight line across the floor and ask players to walk along it. A few drunkards may fall by the wayside after a couple of staggering steps, but the majority will probably manage it reasonably well. Now ask them to repeat the journey, this time looking through the wrong end of a pair of binoculars. Suddenly, it's not as easy... and they begin to wish they hadn't had that tenth can of lager after all.